LITERATURE UNBOUND

"Part literary criticism and part literary
history, the book offers first some lively
interpretations of selected works within a
discussion of various literary types, then
romps through the whole of western
literature touching all the high points and
managing to include biography, social
history, and much else.

"With its wide range and breezy
intelligence it is a useful and delightful
primer on literature."

Kenneth Silverman
Professor of English
New York University

LITERATURE UNBOUND

A Guide for the Common Reader

Sam Tanenhaus

BALLANTINE BOOKS • NEW YORK

For K. B.

ISBN 0-345-33297-0

This edition published by arrangement with Doubleday and Company, Inc.

Manufactured in the United States of America

First Ballantine Books Edition: May 1986

Table of Contents

CONCLUSION:
BEING A READER

Acknowledgments

I am indebted to Greg Tobin for commissioning this book and to the following for reading a primitive version of it and offering invaluable criticism and suggestions: Kathryn Bonomi; Matthew Brennan; Mary Busch; David Cantor; John Chambers; Barbara Greenman; Polly Morrice; Sandy Munro; and Gussie Tanenhaus.

Author's Note

For this edition I have expanded, clarified, and deleted a few paragraphs, rewritten some sentences, and weeded out as many solecisms as I could find, but have not otherwise altered the book's original design and arguments. As before, Part I discusses well-known passages, mostly unidentified within the text (the reader who prefers to know what he's reading when he reads it can refer to Appendix I); and Part II, a quick survey of literary history, supplies basic information about authors and their epochs.

S. T.

"Watch how you enter and in whom you trust."

—*Dante*, INFERNO

PRELUDE:
SONG AND
SENTENCE

20826

Magic and the Spoken Word

Western literature begins with a Greek troubadour born about eight hundred years before Christ. Since the alphabet was then known to only a handful of Greeks, Homer was probably illiterate, which means he composed his famous epics, the *Iliad* and the *Odyssey*, in his head and recited them from memory, a feat inviting skepticism because the briefer of the two, the *Odyssey*, is twelve thousand lines long. Small wonder that in later times Homer's authorship was challenged. Some scholars suggested that the epics were the work of a lettered poet who assembled them from popular folktales; others allowed for an authentically illiterate Homer, but with an altered identity—he was, by their account, one of a band of ancient troubadours equally responsible for the epics, better remembered than his fellows simply because posterity, when it came to record the poems, awarded him sole authorship. Odd that our own century, with its habit of disbelief, should have reestablished the plausibility of the "first" Homer, analphabetic inventor and reciter of the epics: in the 1930s, researchers in the Balkans found illiterate troubadours reeling off without a hitch verses of extreme length and difficulty. A discredited legend abruptly gained new credence: Homer *did* keep those huge poems in his head.

How did he do it? For one thing, he was a singer, aided by melody and rhythm. We attend a reading and the poet has a text before him, but crooners, even in this age of the teleprompter, command repertoires running into the hundreds. Consider how many song lyrics most of us have stored in our heads and how accessible they are; when we're stuck for a phrase we return to the top of the verse, sing it through once more, and memory springs open like a lock, elusive words tumbling free.

Homer's problem was more formidable, of course, and his solution more complex. After all, he sang not only for pleasure but for his supper, and history nowhere records that ancient audiences tolerated interruptions while the bard fished for words. Melody and rhythm, which he provided for himself by plucking a lyre, helped somewhat, as did the structure of the epics. They were made up of separable books, like chapters; as he sang he mentally detached them, one at a time, letting the rest slide momentarily from consciousness. Also, a system of recurrent epithets— instead of "Athena," he sang of "gray-eyed Athena," or "the gray-eyed goddess"—kept the rhythm thumping while he scanned his memory for what came next. Reciting required enormous skill and practice, but, as those Balkan troubadours proved, it could be managed.

It's one thing to carry a poem in your head, another to compose it there, and not just any poem, but an image-drenched epic teeming with characters and incidents. Fortunately, Homer didn't have to invent it all: a great deal of material circulated freely among the oral poets. Homer's special genius was for consolidation. He stitched borrowed fragments along with his own scenes and stories into a fabric grand in its overall design and lush in its particulars, then likely spent years streamlining, revamping, testing out new bits in front of his live audience, as stand-up comics do, gauging what played and what fell flat. His revising led to this:

> *. . . For blows aplenty*
> *awaited me from the god who shakes the earth.*
> *Cross gales he blew, making me lose my bearings,*
> *and heaved up seas beyond imagination—*
> *huge and foundering seas. All I could do*
> *was hold hard, groaning under every shock,*
> *until my craft broke up in the hurricane.*
> *I kept afloat and swam . . . or drifted,*
> *taken by wind and current to this coast*
> *where I went in on big swells running landward.*
> *But cliffs and rock shoals made that place forbidding,*
> *so I turned back, swimming off shore, and came*
> *in the end to a river, to auspicious water,*
> *with smooth beach and a rise that broke the wind.*
> *I lay there where I fell till strength returned.*

5

Then sacred night came on, and I went inland
to high ground and a leaf bed in a thicket.
Heaven sent slumber in an endless tide
submerging my sad heart among the leaves.
That night and next day's dawn and noon I slept;
the sun went west; and then sweet sleep unbound me,
when I became aware of maids . . .
playing along the beach; the princess, too,
most beautiful. I prayed her to assist me,
and her good sense was perfect; one could hope
for no behavior like it from the young,
thoughtless as they most often are. But she
gave me good provender and good red wine,
a river bath, and finally this clothing.
There is the bitter tale. These are the facts.

We can see why the legend of a singing Homer originated and why it persists. There is something spontaneous about these words. The first-person delivery is only part of it. More important is the sublime straightforwardness of the poet's rendering of phenomena. A storm, a thicket, a god—the objectively real and the imagined—are treated equally, as if there's no reason to distinguish between them. This is most evident when the speaker, Odysseus, sober general, veteran of a ten-year siege, employs figures of speech, for instance, "the god who shakes the earth." We envision perhaps a giant wrestling a land mass. "Cross gales he blew": he exhales a hurricane. It's a vivid image, but to Odysseus it's no image at all. He is merely reporting what he has experienced; he even sums up with that familiar, tight-lipped boast, "These are the facts."

6

That "heaven sent slumber" and a god whistles a gale through his teeth? These are facts? To us they seem like metaphors, poetic elaboration. Can it be that for Odysseus and his auditors—and for Homer and his—metaphors *are* facts, that a breath and a storm wind really are the same? To answer this we must reflect on pre-alphabetic concepts, first, of knowledge and second, of language.

For us "knowledge" includes a wide array of information unavailable through direct experience. I "know," for example, that in seven years all the cells in my body will have been replaced. I don't feel this change, but biology tells me it is happening, so I submit to its truth. Call this knowledge *analytic*. "Knowledge" also includes information acquired through sensation—of color, sound, taste, touch, smell. Call this knowledge *perceptual*. In the alphabetic world, perception, with its high quotient of intuition, ranks far below analytic knowledge as a source of truth, but in antiquity their status was reversed. Our prescientific ancestors, lacking reliable investigative instruments, depended on their senses and their sense to achieve a coherent understanding of the world. Odysseus's perception of a storm as a breath writ large is grounded in neither analysis nor fancy; it comes, rather, from his experience of hurricanes, which in terms of sight, sound, and observable effect correspond to his experience of exhalations. Perception, the act of imagination which joins a human breath to a raging storm, provides him with a reasonable account of reality. When he claims to have told "the facts,"

Odysseus is doing, insofar as he is capable, just that.

Now for the role of language in oral literature. Why do Odysseus's listeners accept his metaphorical reading of storms-as-breaths? Because the words he uses conjure up like experiences of their own. Compare a metaphorical "fact" used in our own day: "the sun sets in the west." Although we know the sun does no such thing, we favor the metaphor because it accords with the phenomenon we seem to have witnessed; our figure of speech conspires with perception to override or defy analytic knowledge. But for Odysseus and his auditors metaphors in no way oppose actuality. Language, naming objects both visible (a thicket) and felt (a god), places them within the imagination, summoning them into being.

In our own day words retain this power, though it is much restricted. Prayers and invocations make us feel the presence of holy beings by naming them, and small superstitious remarks like "Good luck" or "Happy birthday" seek to will possibilities into actualities. By and large, however, we resist the incantatory pull of words; we have seen them misused in too many ways; sometimes we even suspect them of misusing us. But in the dawn of culture, when speech was born and poetry with it, words joined the namer and his listener to whatever was named—one man murmured "moon" and no matter the time of day, others felt it. "Gray-eyed Athena" is a name, as is "the god who shakes the earth." Homer, uttering them, threw a switch in the head of his listeners, releasing a thousand fugitive memories.

Logic and the Alphabet

At the same time Homer was raising oral literature to unprecedented heights, other Greeks picked up a new tool from their trading partners, the Phoenicians. The alphabet was at first limited to business transactions (hence generations passed before the *Iliad* and the *Odyssey* were written down, an act of consecration or preservation, like the bottling of wine). We who are weaned on the alphabet seldom reflect on its complexity, but were an oral poet shown a series of markings (h-o-u-s-e) and told they stand for four walls and a roof, would be puzzled indeed. Even someone with a knowledge of the alphabet has to make an infinite mental leap from what sits on the page to what occupies space in the world of objects. These connections suggest the various stages the alphabet itself passed through as it evolved—it began with ideographs, drawings of objects unconnected to their names;

advanced to symbols representing the syllables of spoken words; then broke syllables into their constituent voicings, converted into symbols which became the actual letters, a process that took centuries.

The alphabet moved literature into a new phase, described here by the great Canadian critic Northrop Frye:

> In this second phase language is more individualized, and words become primarily the outward expression of inner thoughts or ideas. Subject and object are becoming more consistently separated, and "reflection," with its overtones of looking into a mirror, moves into the verbal foreground. The intellectual operations of the mind become distinguishable from the emotional operations; hence abstraction becomes possible, and the sense that there are valid and invalid ways of thinking, a sense which is to a degree independent of our feelings, develops into the conception of logic.

A new question arises: why didn't the oral poet's spell crumble under the pressure of analysis? Why don't we balk at heaven "send[ing]" sleep? (On the beak of a bird? By Western Union?) True, Homer's words give as complete and faithful a rendering of reality as was possible in his day, but this merely rationalizes Homer's perspective without accounting for the continued magic of the epics. For an explanation we turn to Aristotle:

> ...our ancestors in the remotest ages have handed down to their posterity traditions in mythical form

10

... that celestial bodies are gods and that the divine encompasses the whole of nature.... For they say that these gods are in the form of men or are like some of the other animals. But if we take only the first essential point, separately from the rest, that the first primary beings are traditionally held to be gods, we may acknowledge that this has been divinely said and that, though arts and philosophies may have been often explored and perfected, but lost, these myths and others have been preserved to the present day like ancient relics. It is only in this way that we can explain and accept the opinions of our ancestors and forerunners.

Analyses fade; metaphors have longevity, because the best of them—myths—have been "divinely said," a phrase which salutes the beauty of metaphors and, as well, suggests that what is beautiful must also be true. Second, myths "have been preserved to the present day," while "arts and philosophies" have been lost. Here we may quarrel. In our day the myths employed by Homer still exist, but only as arcana; philosophical theories postdating Homer by only a few hundred years—Plato's, for instance—are no less well known. But since two millenniums separate us from Aristotle, we may profit by taking him less literally, interpreting him to mean not that the particular myths current in his own era will be preserved forever, "like ancient relics," but that the metaphorical or mythical *outlook* persists. This we can verify by the "setting sun." Isn't it an instance where each of us "loses" philosophical knowledge and "preserves" a myth?

11

With the advent of the alphabet and its legacy of sequential prose, literature was encumbered with new expectations. The latter-day writer, unlike the oral poet, must pass through the fire of knowledge in order to arrive at the imaginative realm. His words—intended, as Homer's weren't, for the page—must be as persuasive and resonant as a speaking voice; at the same time they must startle us out of our accustomed responses, so that things can once again play freshly on our senses. The oral poet bound his listeners to the world by making the strange seem familiar; the writer resituates us in it by making the familiar seem strange.

The next four chapters introduce the reader to versions of reality which rival those put forth by knowledge. They do so not by refusing to accept—acknowledge—the facts, but by exposing facts as inadequate. A prized misconception of our day, a feature of what I call the harsh-reality syndrome, is that the imagination wilts before knowledge, or seeks an "escape." But a hard look at the hegemony of the "arts and philosophies," of science and logical thought, yields an altogether different conclusion: every superseded explanation of the universe, every vanquished theory of human behavior, vindicates the oral poet and his spellbound listeners. For they perceived long ago what knowledge merely confirms, that all truths are metaphors, all discoveries partial, and the only reality is the reality we invent.

PART ONE

THINGS AS THEY ARE:
THE REALISTIC
NOVEL

"The world was different—
whether for worse or for better—
from her rudimentary readings..."

—HENRY JAMES

The New Fiction

On March 31, 1750, Samuel Johnson, the leading critic of his age, published "The Comedy of Romance," an essay prompted by the popular success of a new kind of fiction. What was new about it? First, its stories. Novelists of the preceding two centuries had spun farfetched tales of chivalry and adventure, involving "imaginary castles...a hermit and a wood, a battle and a shipwreck." Now authors are beginning to fashion plots based on actuality, hinging on "accidents that daily happen." Characters, too, have changed. In the old romances they were as fanciful as the events which befell them; those "heroes...traitors, deliverers, and persecutors" were, Dr. Johnson notes, "beings of another species." The new author rejects these stock types, modeling his creations instead on persons found in "the living world." Suddenly fiction, historically in flight from reality, has become its principal record.

This development does not please Dr. Johnson. Absurd as the old romances had been, the lessons they dispensed were sound: good triumphed over evil, chastity was rewarded, courage swept the prizes. Their heroes had been Heroes, their villains Villains. But in 1750 these certitudes are fast disappearing. Protagonists and antagonists consist equally of base and noble traits; and the natural-seeming plots which envelop them, though they mirror the vicissitudes of real life, subvert the harmonious picture of society art is charged with presenting.

To correct this defect, Dr. Johnson prescribes a remedy. Henceforth virtue in fiction should be "the purest that humanity can reach"; and vice

> should always disgust; nor should the graces of gaiety, or the dignity of courage, be so united with it, as to reconcile it to the mind. Wherever it appears, it should raise hatred by the malignity of its practices, and contempt by the meanness of its stratagems.

Fortunately novelists by and large ignored the good doctor. Had they not, our libraries would be bulging with insufferable books. Not that novelists are deaf to the moral imperative. On the contrary, no literary form seems more ethical than the realistic novel: none comments so shrewdly on our lives and values, none wants so badly to teach us. The list of great realistic novelists is, in fact, a roll call of moralists, from Jane Austen to George Eliot to Gustave Flaubert to Leo

Tolstoy to Henry James to Saul Bellow. And they earn the name because of their commitment to the very practices Dr. Johnson deplores: they allow their characters to assume richly diverse, even contradictory shapes, instead of pasting labels on them marked "good" or "bad," and their stories reflect a world that is ambiguous and unpredictable. We turn to realistic writers not because they tell us how things ought to be, but because they show us how things really are.

How did the novel acquire this role, and why in the eighteenth century? For answers we must quickly glance at the genesis of the new fiction, and its prime subject, "the new man."

The New Class

The seeds of the new fiction were sown in the Renaissance, when the centuries-old dominion of a feudal economy began to break down. This happened for numerous reasons, though three stand out: books, thanks to the invention of the printing press, increased in availability, bringing fresh ideas into manorial enclaves; trade routes made rivers and roads safer for travel, emboldening many to explore new turf; and

cities were springing up to accommodate the bur-
geoning population of transients. A large peasant class,
long doomed to tilling the soil or sweating for a pit-
tance at the workbench, responded to these stirrings
of freedom and mobility. Some sailed for distant ports
on merchant ships, others joined trade guilds. Leg-
ends spread of adventurers piling up fortunes and
becoming important *bourgeoisie*, town-dwellers. For
every prosperous adventurer, hundreds, of course,
were dealt stinging blows. The new life could be dangerous and cruel. But gradually enough manufacturers and speculators and traders flourished to form a
new class—the middle class.

The middle class experienced the world as a chancy
place, governed by fortune, fluidity, and flux. Its typ-
ical member, unlike the nobleman, had no esteemed
family name to clear his path, no inherited land pay-
ing rent when business went slack. Nor did he share
the peasant's resignation to a life of limited prospects.
Instead he banked on his wits, his knowledge of how
and when to strike a bargain, and, above all, his conviction that he could make his way in the world.

By 1750, when Dr. Johnson's essay appears, the
middle class is solidly entrenched: speculators and
merchants grip the reins of a madly fluctuating economy; the industrial revolution is only a decade away;
in the next generation two more revolutions, one in
the American colonies, the other in France, will spill
blood in the name of bourgeois individualism. One
last bulwark stands between feudal values and the new
order, class distinctions, and these too are buckling.

20

The upper and lower orders still accept class barriers as a legacy of natural law. But the merchant or financier who has vaulted from poverty to wealth, helplessness to power, can't square this creaky notion with his own experience of the world. Money and political influence, now confidently in his possession, had been equally off limits. If one went about it right, why shouldn't headway be possible in the social game? Not long before, this would have been unthinkable. But in the eighteenth century, with its large and multiplying urban populations, its thickening social texture, the middle class begins to make inroads. To the ranks of the privileged are added a few professionals, who by virtue of superior social graces earn the honorific "gentlemen."

The novelist, unless he left his wits in his inkwell, soon grasped the possibilities of this ferment. Spruce up the heroic romance and he'd have sturdy narrative chassis on which to mount up-to-date chronicles. Characters, for instance, require refurbishing, though the old stock types, those "beings of another species," are not simply discarded: "deliverers" and "persecutors" beget innocents and sharpies; white-throated maidens are still common as sparrows, only now they are ingenues; and it is a persuasive scapegrace, instead of a giant or outlaw knight, who must be fended off. Social combat replaces physical struggle: out go the battlefields and tempests and deserts and woods, in come banks and bedrooms and parlors. Gone are the buried treasures and chalices, supplanted by incomes and deeds of title. The heroic quest had traditionally allegorized the life of the devout Christian whose travails led him from sin to redemption, vice to virtue. This progress of the soul is now applied to the social world, and secularized. No longer does the innocent hero journey toward the sacrament; he aspires instead to bourgeois triumphs such as prosperity and prestige, and in his way stand no absolute evils, only others like himself, though perhaps less good-hearted and open, who either abet or deter him.

The clash of a heroic form with unheroic content is bound to result in comedy, as Dr. Johnson's coinage, "the comedy of romance," makes clear. It further implies that the comic frequently involves ignobility, a condition the new man and his aspirations seem born to. Picture the upstart at a posh dinner party: watching how the other guests handle their forks and position their elbows; devouring with his gaze the table, chandelier, carpets, and objets d'art; taking silent notes during the conversation ("So that's the symphony I should hear"); missing no potential key or clue. Seldom malignant, his deceptions are principally self-deceptions, his blunders committed against himself. He is nonetheless a kind of imposter.

Here is a classic example of the comic realist's method for representing such a poseur. The speaker is a provincial clergyman proposing to the lady of his choice:

"Allow me, by the way, to observe, my fair cousin, that I do not reckon the notice and kindness of [my patron] Lady Catherine de Bourgh as among the least of the advantages in my power to offer. You will find her manners beyond any thing I can describe... Thus much for my general intention in favor of matrimony; it remains to be told why my views were directed to Longbourn...the fact is, that being, as I am, to inherit this estate after the death of your honoured father, (who, however, may live many years longer,) I could not satisfy myself without resolving to chuse a wife from among his daughters, that the loss to them might be as little as possible, when the melancholy event takes place— which, however, as I have already said, may not be for several years.... And now nothing remains for me but to assure you in the most animated language of the violence of my affection. To fortune I am perfectly indifferent, and shall make no demand of that nature on your father, since I am well aware that it could not be complied with; and that one thousand pounds in the 4 per cents. which will not be yours till after your mother's decease, is all that you may ever be entitled to. On that head, therefore, I shall be uniformly silent; and you may assure yourself that no ungenerous reproach shall ever pass my lips when we are married."

The clergyman is pompous, snobbish, manipulative, materialistic, insensitive, and perhaps incapable of love. Yet the author never expressly says so. We divine these attributes from the character's own stilted locutions. We notice that his "violent affection" is forgotten in the instant it's mentioned, no doubt to his "fair" cousin's relief, and that he dwells with unwitting cruelty on the possible demise of her father, and on the likelihood of her becoming destitute. In every phrase we sense the hand of the author, giving the words an ironic spin, placing contradictions and absurdities within an entirely plausible contest—without intruding into the text; the character speaks for himself. As a report on social conditions the passage is no less exemplary. We learn that, some two hundred years ago, a man's estate did not pass on to his daughters; that the conditions of one's finances were a matter of public knowledge and comment; that matrimony routinely depended on external factors, chiefly money. This information is not laid out for us, but if we read with care we can't miss it.

Buffoon this character may be, and a disgrace to the clerical collar, but we do not wish him other than he is; nor does his author, who takes evident delight in him, lovingly setting forth every disagreeable trait. No artist can dislike what he, or in this case she, has studied so diligently and reinvented with such relish. There is, moreover, something innately appealing about this imposter: he acts not out of cynical knowledge of the world but its opposite, the bungler's misconception of "how things are done." He is, like the hypothetical upstart at the dinner party, an innocent.

Comic realism was indebted to the new man, both for observing the pretenses of those on the rungs above him and for his shameless attempts to copy them. He uncovered a crucial truth about society: when lineage counts for little, who you are becomes a matter of what you seem. In this way all social beings, not just frauds and manipulators, are impersonators. We acknowledge this today when we speak of "roles."

We have roles on the job, at home, and in public. These don't conflict with our true identities; each, rather, contains a germ of ourselves. Children play dress-up; young poets smoke Gauloises; the new man aped those more accomplished than himself. In so doing he aimed not only to get somewhere, but to become something. His journey, though set in a resoundingly material world, was spiritual; his desire, underneath his materialistic shell, was to transform himself.

What Seems and What Is

It was inevitable that a literary form which vividly captured the aspirations of the middle class should find among its ranks a loyal following, and eighteenth-century readers are legendary for their passionate involvement in novels. They clamored for new volumes, queued up for fresh installments of those already in print (it was the custom then to serialize long works); some pounded on the doors of authors, demanding to know what fate awaited the hero or heroine currently in fashion. It was not merely the seduction of a good story that drove them to such lengths. The authentic surfaces in realistic novels, their accurate detailing of manners and habits, held clues for those upstarts who had not yet made it into polite society. By studying the adventures of Samuel Richardson's Clarissa Harlowe or Henry Fielding's Tom Jones, readers apprenticed themselves to these fictional blood kin, and

> fix their eyes upon [them] with closer attention, and hope, by observing [their] behavior and success, to regulate their own practices, when they shall be engaged in the like part.

Dr. Johnson, forlorn witness of social flux, saw that an odd reversal had occurred. Comic realists, who had begun as students of human manners, were now becoming authorities, and, worse, their creations, intended to be copies, served as models. This was potentially a bonus, so long as the novelist sat in responsible judgment of the social spectacle, pointing readers toward Good and away from Evil. But as the doctor lamented and we have seen, authors rejected this office. As faithful chroniclers of the actual they could not simply stride into a text and start bossing around characters who must be left, as in life, to the fates dictated by probability. Authors could interpolate sermons and warnings and admonitions, and some did, usually with a humorous twist, but generally they relied on quieter ways of commenting on character and event. For the reader schooled in literary subtleties this strategy presented no problem. But

> these books are written chiefly to the young, the ignorant, and the idle, to whom they serve as lectures of conduct, and introductions into life. They are the entertainment of minds unfurnished with ideas, and therefore easily susceptible of impressions; not fixed by principles, and therefore easily following the current of fancy; not informed by experience, and consequently open to every false suggestion and partial account.

Dr. Johnson had little faith in the common reader, and probably, judging from the way novels were swallowed rather than read, he was justified. This put the author in a strange position. The novel is essentially a didactic form. Even the "comedy of romance," with its reportorial interest in the look and feel of things, and its mask of impartiality, sought to teach. How does a genre whose popularity is based on sympathy for the new man—not necessarily for his actions, but his outlook—enlighten him? Dr. Johnson understood the problem (there is little about the novel his essay doesn't understand, strict as its verdicts seem), but the solution eluded him. He urged a retreat into old literary practices, the two-column approach, one side titled "good" (courage, chastity, piety, probity, etc.), the other "bad" (cowardice, promiscuity, irreverence, dishonesty, etc.), an arrangement bound to fail because it smacked of the old feudal rigidity. No author who endorsed it could expect much of a readership.

The writer's only choice was to make the material world, presented realistically, the stage for moral progress: the upstart had not only to achieve his bourgeois dream, he must become a better person. The realist capitalized on the identification of protagonist and reader, uniting both as active readers of things as they are, so that the march through time and events, up peaks and down valleys gradually revealed the materialistic point of view—the world perceived as concrete realities—to be thoroughly unreliable.

Pride and Prejudice, from which the clergyman's speech comes, describes such a journey. On the face of it, the novel has almost no action, or, rather, the action is restricted to small and ordinary episodes. But to most readers it seems a wonderful and perilous adventure. We take the part of its charming heroine, Elizabeth Bennet, and feel ourselves to grow and learn with her. She is not larger than life, nor an overflowing fountain of emotion, but a self-confessed reader of "intricate characters." (No wonder the clergyman doesn't spark her interest.) She studies her family and relatives and friends and several suitors, always arriving at subtle interpretations which are, with startling consistency, wrong. An example: the clergyman, quickly rebounding from her flat rejection, proposes to her best friend, a paragon of good sense who, to Elizabeth's amazement and consternation, accepts. Her friend's sudden irrationality is troubling, to us no less than Elizabeth. How could she tolerate a lifetime of unctuousness and pomposity, or be taken in by fraudulent assurances of violent affection? We overlook every explanation but the most obvious, that to someone with scant prospects the clergyman is a respectable catch. The character's good sense has not forsaken her; it has, rather, enabled her to do what Elizabeth, at this early stage, can't, measure things as they are from more than a single perspective.*

The main event in *Pride and Prejudice* is the gradual evolution of the heroine's opinion of the aristocratic Mr. Darcy, whom she has pegged from the outset as one kind of man, though he turns out to be quite another. Jane Austen's lesson is not a pious "Don't judge by appearances," but, contrarily, that we are doomed to misread because we have only appearances to judge by. Learning the truth, that Mr. Darcy is a sensitive gentleman, is less important than learning that the truth can only be arrived at through misapprehension. It is not revealed to us; we must evolve toward it, and still we may miss it, even when it grins at us. An illusion we are all loath to part with is that once the truth swims into view all uncertainties van-

---

*Here is a place where serious realism departs from formulaic realism. In the latter, the person who doesn't marry "for love" has made a grave error, and sooner or later (we wait for it like vultures) "pays the price." But where, outside our fantasies, do any marriages prove ideal? What happens to love when it's depleted of passion? When Mr. or Ms. Right is revealed in his or her fallibility? Do we look for someone else to marry "for love," or do we (unless we're movie stars) reexamine ourselves and our conception of what love itself is?

ish.† The comic romancer knows, however, that we seldom locate the final, conclusive fact; and even when we do we sometimes fail to recognize it.

Illusion Equals Truth

In the nineteenth century the middle class and the novel reached their apogee as bourgeois values and habits were standardized (even the upper classes becoming, so to speak, middle-class). But the new man did not coast on his glory. He now decided that his stupendous journey had been sacramental, after all, and set about converting his personal creed into a religion, its church material success, its priests capitalists, its flock stretching from the Thames to the

---

†This explains the appeal of melodrama. Once the killer is unmasked, the money returned to the bank, the skeleton dragged out of the closet, all the confusion neatly ends. Melodrama always unfolds in a crisis atmosphere of multiplying disasters; this serves to make the condition of doubt seem exceptional and remote. The masters of melodrama achieve powerful effects by telling their stories in flat, almost toneless prose, so that the implausible becomes ironically synonymous with the ordinary.

Congo. He resuscitated quaint code words, like chastity and piety, and added new ones, like earnestness and industriousness. The comic romance was solemnized as the novel, its prestige as a literary form for the first time rivaling that of poetry, from which it seized the epic mantle. Tales, instead of recounting a few years in a hero's life, sprawled over generations; some ambitious authors documented whole epochs in multiple, linked novels researched as exhaustively as biological treatises. Its authority as the record of society thoroughly vindicated, the novel assayed a bolder didacticism in its reading of social reality, and there was evident need for it: public life held out more deceptions and confusing appearances than ever before. Genuine understanding, sought by all, was a triumph attained by the select few.

A classic example of the nineteenth-century novel and its mingling of material and spiritual growth is Charles Dickens's *Great Expectations*. It tells how the orphaned narrator Pip, through the auspices of an anonymous benefactor, is plucked from his apprenticeship to a blacksmith and sent to London where he is fashioned into a gentleman. From the outset Pip has an inkling of his benefactor's identity: it must be Miss Havisham, the bitter old woman who has taken an inexplicable interest in him. From her and her young ward, Estella, Pip first learns that the social world splits into two kingdoms, the "common," poor unwashed types like the blacksmith and his wife, and the "uncommon," like Miss Havisham and Estella, with Pip himself a borderline figure, a temporary dweller among the common with unmistakable attributes of the un-.‡

Though Pip is an orphan, his ancestry is long and illustrious. He is heir to the archetypal bourgeois of the late Middle Ages, blessed with luck, intelligence, a pleasing countenance, and deeper virtues—hope and the will to reinvent himself. Dr. Johnson described such a character as "an adventurer ... levelled with the rest of the world, [who] acts in such scenes of the universal drama, as may be the lot of any other man." In an age of bourgeois preeminence the ordinary man is the exemplary man. Where does spirituality enter? For one thing Pip, the ideal Victorian aspirant, is no pulled-up-by-his-own-bootstraps hero. His assault on polite society is arranged without his lifting a single scheming finger; he is *summoned* to the call of upward mobility, and by a force both invisible and potent (even if its agent appears to be a cranky old dowager). Next, Pip fervently believes that he is destined for higher things and that becoming a gentleman is tantamount to a reincarnation. Finally, like all true questers he is animated by love. Estella, whom he woos in his dreams, is his golden chalice. No ambitious *bourgeois* was ever more spiritualized.

---

‡The hero whose inner nobility shines through humble garb is an ancient convention, extending back to Homer. In the age of literacy it can result in implausibilities. Dickens was not the only novelist to permit his heroes, even when born to poverty and ignorance, to speak a barrister's English. Today, in America, this defect is generally limited to subliterary forms. The white-Stetsoned "deliverer" in Westerns, for example, often speaks like, and sometimes is, a college graduate.

Pip has more at stake than the heroes of comic romances; like Elizabeth Bennet he undergoes self-revision, but the cost seems greater and the ironies crueler, particularly when he discovers he has misidentified his patron. Enter Abel Magwitch, a former convict whom Pip encountered long ago in a grim incident he has tried to forget, though it has been the fulcrum of Magwitch's reformation. Pip is *his* golden chalice:

> "Yes, Pip, dear boy, I've made a gentleman on you! It's me wot has done it! I swore that time, sure as ever I earned a guinea, that guinea should go to you. I swore arterwards, sure as ever I spec'lated and got rich, you should get rich. I lived rough, that you should live smooth; I worked hard that you should be above work. What odds, dear boy? Do I tell it fur you to feel a obligation? Not a bit. I tell it, fur you to know as that there hunted dunghill dog wot you kep life in, got his head so high that he could make a gentleman—and, Pip, you're him."

Learning the truth, Pip recoils, absorbing this revelation, not as an alert reader of reality, but with the pious distaste of the arriviste. He doesn't ponder for a moment the many ironies of his great expectations, for instance, that they are not great but commonplace (even Magwitch is a votary of the Victorian creed) and that since it is money and not inner merit which makes a poor boy a gentleman, status is for sale; the specific well from which the lucre is drawn is nearly beside the point. To his benefactor and surrogate father he shows no gratitude or affection. In fact it's all he can do to quell his revulsion. He recognizes in Magwitch neither teacher nor fellow aspirant. From the summit of his respectability (purchased by Magwitch in sweat and pain and loneliness and risk) he spies only a villain. His spiritual education has been spotty indeed.

For Dickens, status is no guarantor of advancement, but rather a shell or vessel which enlightened perception must fill with meaning. Pip, until his moment of renunciation, succeeds in this effort. Because he perceives himself as reincarnated, he acts as if he is, and therefore *has* reincarnated himself. When he loses his gift of imaginative perception he becomes just another protagonist, a callow leading man. The distance he falls measures the heights he might have attained.

The Journey Inward

The nineteenth century restored religion to the novel, but it was a religion Dr. Johnson could not have foreseen. True, his lexicon of virtues was back in vogue. Today everyone knows how in the Victorian era sexual restraint and moral purity were preached in the pulpits, in the classroom, and in hundreds of execrable novels. Even a titan like Dickens was infected, and never portrayed a heroine who wasn't a radiant improbability. Dr. Johnson would have approved. But beneath the superficial proprieties Dickens's fiction swells with dark discovery. Angels wear prison stripes; illusions sink their roots in dunghills. A mere sensationalist would content himself with ripping away the veil, baring the ugly leer of the truth. Dickens's revelations, as we've seen, are trickier. One's patron may have a tainted past, but his vision can be as immaculate as a banker's. Like Jane Austen, Dickens observed that truth derives its meaning from illusion. Magwitch's surprise wouldn't erase Pip's illusions if he didn't have them. Nor would Mr. Darcy's true nature tip Elizabeth Bennet's head if she hadn't fabricated, through the false logic of misreadings, an altogether different impression.

Our relation to reality is never inert; it is our fate to act on what we think we know. This is what makes the heroes of realism believable. Like ourselves, they plunge into error on the wrong evidence, or evidence badly digested. In the benignly patterned universe of *Pride and Prejudice* all the wrinkles can be smoothed; in *Great Expectations* the flaws seem stitched into the pattern itself; society is schismatically rent, not along the simple lines Pip first discerned (common versus uncommon) but in an obscure, riddling way that can never be mended.

* * *

The realist of our own century is a psychologist, less interested in the contours of reality than in the inner dynamics of seeing, the process by which we learn to read surfaces and appearances. He too unteaches us, and more radically than his predecessors because he has jettisoned even their standards of measurement; "truth" and "appearance," "reality" and "illusion" no longer apply when every meaning is approximate, every discovery provisional.

Here is a passage from *Swann's Way*, the first novel in Marcel Proust's monumental cycle, *A la Recherche du Temps Perdu*, translated into English as *Remembrance of Things Past*:

> Swann, who never spoke of his brilliant connections, but only of those...he would have considered it snobbish to conceal, and among whom he had come to include his connections in the official world, [said]..."I happen to be lunching with the Prefect of Police to-morrow at the Elysée."
>
> "What's that? The Elysée?" Dr Cottard roared in a voice of thunder.
>
> "Yes, at M. Grévy's," replied Swann, a little embarrassed at the effect which his announcement had produced.

As a rule, once an explanation had been given, Cottard would say: "Ah, good, good; that's all right, then," after which he would show not the least trace of emotion. But this time Swann's last words, instead of the usual calming effect, had that of raising to

36

fever-pitch his astonishment at the discovery that a man with whom he himself was actually sitting at table, a man who had no official position, no honours or distinction of any sort, was on visiting terms with the Head of State.

"What's that you say? M. Grévy? You know M. Grévy?" he demanded of Swann, in the stupid and incredulous tone of a constable on duty at the palace who, when a stranger asks to see the President of the Republic, realising at once "the sort of man he is dealing with," as the newspapers say, assures the poor lunatic that he will be admitted at once, and directs him to the reception ward of the police infirmary.

"I know him slightly; we have some friends in common" (Swann dared not add that one of these friends was the Prince of Wales). "Besides, he is very free with his invitations, and I assure you his luncheon-parties are not the least bit amusing. They're very simple affairs, too, you know—never more than eight at table," he went on, trying desperately to cut out everything that seemed to show off his relations with the President in a light too dazzling for the doctor's eyes.

Whereupon Cottard, at once conforming in his mind to the literal interpretation of what Swann was saying, decided that invitations from M. Grévy were very little sought after, were sent out, in fact, into the highways and byways. And from that moment he was no longer surprised to hear that Swann, or anyone else, was "always at the Elysée"; he even felt a little sorry for a man who had to go to luncheon-parties which he himself admitted were a bore.

In this next sentence, which opens the second novel, *Within a Budding Grove*, the narrator shrugs off the omniscient voice and speaks in his own person:

37

My mother, when it was a question of our having M. de Norpois to dinner for the first time, having expressed her regret that Professor Cottard was away from home and that she herself had quite ceased to see anything of Swann, since either of these might have helped to entertain the ex-ambassador, my father replied that so eminent a guest, so distinguished a man of science as Cottard could never be out of place at a dinner-table, but that Swann, with his ostentation, his habit of crying aloud from the house-tops the name of everyone he knew, however slightly, was a vulgar show-off whom the Marquis de Norpois would be sure to dismiss as— to use his own epithet—a "pestilent" fellow.

Everything the reader has learned is abruptly turned inside out, like an umbrella in a windstorm. Swann a "vulgar show-off"? Cottard an "eminent guest...never out of place at a dinner-table"? Where did we misread? How were we misled? Has the author himself forgotten the true nature of his characters? As with any good story we long to be filled in, to find out what happened, although, in this novel obsessed with temporality (its title literally translates as "in search of lost time"), consequence precedes cause. In literature and in life we ultimately pursue, not conclusions, but beginnings. How was the universe formed, how did species originate, what caused the fall of Rome? The present we feel as we live it; the future recedes as it approaches, like happiness and mirages; but the past is curiously alive. Thus the amnesiac's obsession with what happened yesterday and the day before, his ceaseless burrowing back. He can't know who he is until he grasps who he used to be. Proust's ropy sentence, with its casual obliteration of an edifice raised by hundreds of pages of development and detail, forces a crisis of amnesia on readers, as if we, no less than Swann and Cottard, had been ambushed and robbed of our identity.

The impact of Proust's revelations is such impact that to speak of them as different from or less than those registered in our own lives seems an insult, to us and to him. He dispels for good another symptom of the harsh-reality syndrome, the crackpot notion that what we read is somehow apart from what we experience. A critic once wrote that when readers learn of reversals in *Remembrance of Things Past*—Swann and Cottard's is but one instance—"the astonishment, the disgust, the deep and actual sorrow that follow are almost comic, so closely do they approximate in degree the emotions the same event in 'actual life' would cause." The quotation marks surrounding "actual life" are illuminating.

I have called Proust a psychologist. By this I don't mean only that he pokes around in the unconscious; novelists had been doing that for generations. What particularly engages Proust is cognition, the process by which perception is converted into knowledge. His narrator, "Marcel," is perhaps the most scrupulous reader of reality in all of literature. The minutest external change—the addition of words to a character's vocabulary, a facial expression new to his repertoire, a novel gesture—sparks prolonged rumination on the impossibility of knowing others. Proust repeatedly demonstrates that our selves are not single but innumerable, with an inexhaustible capacity for change. In our attempt to understand one another we are like satellites spinning around planets, subject and object, see-er and seen, in constant revision.

Thus the "spatial" discoveries in Proust. Space, as Einstein taught us, is continuous with time. So is it in this great novel. Consider, again, Swann and Cottard and their peculiarly reversed status. As we weigh what they are "now" against our remembrance of what they used to be, both impressions are modified. Time changes them, not by erasing what they once were, but by superimposing new selves on the old. Moreover, we readers, having ourselves evolved, are disqualified from conclusively assessing the change. We "search" vainly for what we ourselves really are.

Our nemesis is time, against which we have a single ally, memory, and even it betrays us. For though memory enables us to hold in our minds two actualities that otherwise would be mutually exclusive (Cottard as he is now, and as he used to be), it also keeps alive all we would choose to forget. We can see how this extends and complicates the matter of appearance and reality, or illusion and truth. No longer do we simply revise a misreading (as, when we were surrogate Elizabeth Bennets, we revised faulty readings of Mr. Darcy, and as Pips, of our mysterious benefactor). For the modern realist perceptions are never overcome or outgrown; instead they thrash against the walls of memory. Total self-transformation is impossible, after all. Our spiritual voyage leads us back to our beginnings.

For all the thickness of social detail in *Remembrance of Things Past*, its drama is interior. In this, as subsequent decades of fiction verify, Proust was a pioneer. Today's realist regards the world of banks and bedrooms and parlors with the same distrust reserved two centuries ago for deserts and woods and castles. This is sometimes interpreted as a rejection of, or disillusionment with, the social world. The message is baffling. Social ferment hasn't slackened; why should the realist lose interest? Perhaps because what were formerly challenges to convention have seized the scepter and imposed a suffocating rule of their own. In its infancy, realism endorsed bourgeois ideals. This seemed reasonable enough. Social flux had its redemptions. The upstart might be an impersonator or, worse, a manipulator, but he was an agent of liberation; the author in the late twentieth century is likely to wonder what this liberation has yielded:

…he let the entire world press upon him. For instance? Well, for instance, what it means to be a man. In a city. In a century. In transition. In a mass. Transformed by science. Under organized power. Subject to tremendous controls. In a condition caused by mechanization. After the late failure of radical hopes. In a society that was no community and devalued the person. Owing to the multiplied power of numbers which made the self negligible. Which spent military billions against foreign enemies but would not pay for order at home. Which permitted savagery and barbarism in its own great cities. At the same time, the pressure of human millions who have discovered what concerted efforts and thoughts can do. As megatons of water shape

41

organisms on the ocean floor. As tides polish stones. As winds hollow cliffs. The beautiful supermachinery opening a new life for innumerable mankind. Would you deny them the right to exist? Would you ask them to labor and go hungry while you enjoyed delicious old-fashioned Values? You—you yourself are a child of this mass and a brother to all the rest. Or else an ingrate, dilettante, idiot. There, Herzog, thought Herzog, since you ask for the instance, is the way it runs.

How Saul Bellow's Herzog struggles to believe that the human race is not a disaster! His optimistic arguments remind one of the maxim that the first "proof" of God's existence tolled the death of faith. When Herzog reflects on men "in a mass...Under organized power. Subject to tremendous controls," the old feudal hierarchy reels into view, except that "science," "mechanization," and "supermachinery," belong to the modern era. Does the progress of society mirror that of the individual, circling back to its origins?

A century ago Dickens well understood that the old religion, the dedication to overarching beliefs, never dies, for in the moment we proclaim the final settling of our account with a mysterious and oppressive "past" we submit to some new pretense to ultimate truth. One epoch's feudalism becomes the mercantilism of the next and then industrial capitalism and then technocracy. Even those who resist the trend are implicated. Herzog, no misty-eyed votary of the official religion, risks—what is equally deplorable—misanthropy, his "delicious old-fashioned Values" a portcullis lowered over his heart. A man of insight, he diagnoses the ailment, testing out epithets—"ingrate, dilettante, idiot"—as cures. But those names are like butter on a burn, the pain numbed without the wound being healed. The same applies to his little lyric about polished stones and hollowed cliffs. He is temporizing, singing a sacral song to ocean and wind as the storm they have brewed sweeps landward.

MYSELF AM HELL:
THE DIVIDED SELF
IN LITERATURE

"The individual does actually
carry on a double existence: one
designed to serve his own
purposes and another as a link in
a chain, in which he serves
against, or at any rate without,
any volition of his own."

—*SIGMUND FREUD*

The Divided Self

What, exactly, *is* society? The Social Studies or Civics blackboard rises in the mind, bannered with the question, only it is no question but a Pavlovian bell, cuing specific salivations: "Institutions"; "Rituals"; "Beliefs." In the next chapter we'll encounter society defined as a "ceremony of innocence," a melodic phrase that requires and will receive, explication. For now let's simply appropriate its first word. Ceremony: wafer and wine; bride, groom, and altar; the coffin winched into the grave. Society means communal order and harmony and decorum, in Dr. Johnson's terms; in Herzog's, system. Both have in mind the absorption of the individual into the public mainstream or, in a phrase of W. H. Auden's, the "Generalised Life."

Realists, we have seen, dedicated their powers to chronicling this process. The hero's project of reinvention involved a series of initiations; every scuttled illusion furthered his understanding of how things really are. With this understanding the bourgeois aspirant won a place in the world. He belonged. And if belonging involved quick changes of identities and roles, it also rewarded him with new selves, each expressive of an inner quality that now had room to flourish. The passages by Proust and Bellow challenged this view. They suggested that the single true self we possess is an inner self, which the process of absorption erodes.

How does society look in this passage?

Carl sipped the cream soda and watched the bubbles in the pipe. They reminded him of bubbles rising from a diving helmet. He imagined a lagoon and schools of remarkable fish.

Jack passed the tube.

Carl stood up and stretched.

"Where are you going, honey?" Mary asked.

"No place," Carl said. He sat down and shook his head and grinned. "Jesus."

Helen laughed.

"What's funny?" Carl said after a long, long time.

"God, I don't know," Helen said. She wiped her eyes and laughed again, and Mary and Jack laughed.

After a time Jack unscrewed the top of the water pipe and blew through one of the tubes. "It gets plugged sometimes."

"What did you mean when you said I was on a bummer?" Carl said to Mary.

"What?" Mary said.

Carl stared at her and blinked. "You said something about me being on a bummer. What made you say that?"

"I don't remember now, but I can tell when you are," she said. "But please don't bring up anything negative, okay?"

"Okay," Carl said. "All I'm saying is I don't know

48

why you said that. If I wasn't on a bummer before
you said it, it's enough when you say it to put me
on one."

Beneath this plain prose tension is gathering. The
occasion for pleasure has become a crisis. The "negative" subject is quelled like an uprising; and when
Carl stands up to stretch, Mary's presentiment—is he
leaving, not only the room, but herself, possibly for
good?—hangs in the air like an unfinished phrase.
Even their laughter rasps grimly over the spaces
between them. If they possessed the talent for imper-
sonation, for pretending, that once formed the basis
of social communion, these two couples might feel
less oppressed. Jane Austen's clergyman, Dickens's
Magwitch, Proust's team of Cottard and Swann, all
had a touch of vaudeville. They burlesqued themselves. But when every word and gesture is saturated
with implied meaning the only relief is silence. One
must be an imposter to get along with others.

For the realist, imposture does not imply dishonesty: our careers, our manners, our habits of speech—
the perpetual donning of roles—contribute to the
formation of our actual selves. But what if this is a
lie? What if the real Carl and Mary are hidden from
us, and each other, by their public gesticulations?
Proust maintained that our real life unfolds in the
secret recesses of the mind. And Saul Bellow suggested that social forces conspire against the "person."
Both point to the existence of another self, possessed
by us all, which in outrage at the "Generalised Life"

is enthralled by a misanthropic wish to terminate the social nexus. Not for reasons or orneriness or perversity, but out of genuine terror. Submitting to the whim of others means policing ourselves. This is what we call "the reality principle," which schools us to accept the paradox that what we secretly crave jeopardizes our well-being. There are those among us who can't accept the limitations imposed by this fact of life; for them desire, the inner calculus of want and need, won't be tamed by common sense. They are thus faced with a dilemma: do they heed the call of secret yearnings, chancing madness or prison or death, or submit to the sanctions of approved social conduct, betraying themselves?

Such a person is likely to suffer greatly in the social world. Not as the realistic hero suffers, for having guessed wrong, or for investing too much in an illusion. Those disappointments are way stations to enlightenment: the hero learns a lesson. For the characters in the above passage, any participation in the world of others endangers their sense of who they are. Yet, and this is what makes their existence painful and absurd, the social impulse flourishes in them; it is part of their human equipment. They are thus divided selves, pulled in two directions.

Our topic, broadly, is psychological literature, or literature of the mind. The psychological author makes us feel like eavesdroppers on an inner dialogue. As in the above passage, the drama lies not in what is plainly spoken or done but in the cauldron of meanings and implications simmering below what "happens." Occasionally a clue bubbles up, as when Carl gives utterance to his "negative" feeling of anger. More often intimations of dread or interior disarray are pressed from view. In the previous chapter we became scrupulous readers of appearances, putting suppositions about reality to the test. We now must learn to sound the depths. Divided selves belong to the earliest Western literature. Homer's Achilles, so-called rebel without a cause, is a divided self. And no one states the dilemma of inner dividedness more forcefully than Hamlet, who can't decide whether "to be or not to be."

"To be or not to be" may be substituted for other, equally stark and final choices, notably between madness and sanity, or criminality and proper conduct. Already the difficulties are apparent: what inner principle can the negative possibly serve? This chapter will look for answers to that riddle and to other no simpler ones. Because they must be explored in detail, I have limited myself to the single dilemma posed by Hamlet. Nearly all the following passages portray persons on the verge of suicide, though we are seldom treated to Hamlet's explicitness—the "negative" is not always named. We may initially have trouble surmising that the "voice" in a particular passage is on the brink of extinction. The speaker may limit his complaint to petty grievances, in no way signifying that his demise is imminent. Suicides in "actual life" are the same way. "I really thought he'd come around," says the confused friend, or, "She was happier than she'd been for months." Strategies for survival, for outwitting the demon, can seem equally irrational. A fantasy or dream of suicide, for example, may actually thwart the death wish by granting the mind that dreams it the psychic satisfaction of having "done it." Another deceptive method is to turn despair on its head, celebrating it as an exalted state of being, substituting a paean to the abyss for a headlong leap.

Fantasy and exaltation require tenacious minds capable of converting anguish into an occasion for creativity. Most divided selves lack such gaudy gifts. Writers have not overlooked the ungifted; neither shall we. They, after all, are most like ourselves, bending under the load of dismay. We all nurture impulses which promise freedom from the demands of others, even if that freedom means death. Divided selves differ from us only in the unrelieved pressure the "negative" exerts on their lives.

The Secret Self

Here are two interior monologues.

(A)

> *Thus play I in one person many people,*
> *And none contented. Sometimes am I king:*
> *Then treasons make me wish myself a beggar,*
> *And so I am. Then crushing penury*
> *Persuades me I was better when a king;*
> *Then am I kinged again; and by and by*
> *Think that I am unkinged...*
> *And straight am nothing. But whate'er I be,*
> *Nor I, nor any man that but man is,*
> *With nothing shall be pleased till he be eased*
> *With being nothing....*

(B)

There will certainly be no one to blame if I should
kill myself, even if the immediate cause should for
instance appear to be F.'s behavior. Once, half asleep,

I pictured the scene that would ensue if, in anticipation of the end, the letter of farewell in my pocket, I should come to her house, should be rejected as a suitor, lay the letter on the table, go to the balcony, break away from all those who run up to hold me back, and, forcing one hand after another to let go its grip, jump over the ledge. The letter, however, would say that I was jumping because of F., but that even if my proposal had been accepted nothing essential would have been changed for me. My place is down below, I can find no other solution, F. simply happens to be the one through whom my fate is made manifest; I can't live without her and must jump, yet—and this F. suspects—I couldn't live with her either. Why not use tonight for the purpose, I can already see before me the people talking at the parents' gathering this evening, talking of life and the conditions that have to be created for it—but I cling to abstractions, I live completely entangled in life, I won't do it, I am cold, am sad that a shirt collar is pinching my neck, am damned, gasp for breath in the mist.

Each voice articulates the allure of suicide. Voice A finds life too volatile: one moment he's on top; then foul play drags him down. Should his spirits and status revive, despair returns on cue, reducing him to a cipher. But—painful irony—he is a nothing who breathes and suffers, who, despite himself, incontestably *is*. At which point the relative "ease" of actual extinction seems a welcome prospect. This intricate line of reasoning has too much wit, wordplay, and vigor to be exactly suicidal, a point even more evident in the case of Voice B.

He finds the suicide proposition funny. Take his first sentence: "There will certainly be no one to blame if I should kill myself, even if the immediate cause should for instance appear to be F.'s behavior." That sly "for instance," deflating the stoical resignation of "no one to blame," launches a sardonic fantasy. In the next sentence— a single sentence!—he outlines the "scene that would ensue" in the event he indulged his wild impulse. It reads like a shooting script for a silent comedy. Hero bursts into boudoir, drops onto one knee, removes hat, slicks hair, dissolves into a groveling heap at the feet of F. She, unmoved, eyes fixed on her nails, levels an imperious finger toward the door and the suitor slinks away, depositing a huge letter on her table. Then, tearing his hand from the doorknob, he reverses direction and charges across the room, jumping with both feet onto the windowsill. F. puts a hand to her astonished mouth, and burly men swarm into the boudoir, grabbing at the ankles of the spurned lover, who sways forty stories above a vehicle-choked boulevard, frozen with fear. At last he teeters into the crowd of waiting arms, and his limp body is carried past the serene F. (who's back at her nails), down the stairs, and outside, where he's dumped onto the pavement, in the rain. In the version scripted by B, however, the boffo lover leaps. The comic and the terrible live side by side. Of course he doesn't really end it all. How can he when he's "completely entangled in" life and its contradictions? His appreciation of the absurd keeps him alive.

The contrast between these voices and the protagonists of realistic fiction is pronounced. Yet their experiences, their opportunities for advancement and enlightenment are equivalent. Consider A's remark that he "play[s]...in one person many people." Is the same not true for realism's impersonators, those protean adopters of roles and appearances? They, as we learned, benefit from the social fray: it shapes their identities, adds to their store of self-knowledge, guides them toward discovering suitable social stations. But A is a reluctant player; his roles are thrust upon him. Each change of identity, from king to beggar and back, confuses and abrades his illusion of autonomy. For B any relation to others, including the woman he loves, is necessarily grotesque. The urge to bid this life goodbye is no mere affectation in these voices; both are rich with real complaint.

Selfishness, thinking only of ourselves, is a condition which, like Herzog, we warn ourselves against. But when we examine the life esteemed by society at large we must seriously wonder whether selfishness is so deserving of scorn. Isn't its true opposite, not unselfishness, but selflessness, a negative condition? Rocks are selfless, and trees and plants. To be selfless means not to have a self. And what but our sense of self differentiates us from what we're not? There is much to be said for cultivating our selfishness, or, if the word still rankles, our *selfness*. This can be accomplished only if we clear our minds of all that is not our*self*, all that is extrinsic and thereby hostile. And first to go is not the furniture of reality—stones and sky—but our fellow lodgers, Others. It is they who burden us with expectations and obligations; they who want to "share" our thoughts and feelings; they who insist on being acknowledged and taken into account. No wonder suicide makes people more angry than sad. The person who takes his life leaves others behind.

Voices A and B, however, step back from the ledge. No one talks them out of it. There is no cop stretching out a brotherly hand; no bear hug for the great big beautiful world which "suddenly seems like a different place." Instead they invent alternative, rival worlds, which they inhabit and rule alone. Voice A withdraws into a secret, inviolable recess of intellect, mordantly assessing the damage sustained in the public world. B confects a mad drama in which he is both actor and audience, even the woman he loves stuck with a secondary part, brought on stage merely to speed him along to his "fate." Megalomania, or narcissism, enables these voices to accomplish creatively what we customarily associate with destruction, the obliteration of others.

To the journey outward made by the first heroes of realism, and the inward route traced by Proust, we can add another, a downward spiral into the pit of the self. This next passage, spoken by a voice from "underground," describes the peculiar triumph and power that ensue

from the too intense consciousness of your own degradation; ... that you yourself felt that you had reached the last barrier; that it was horrible, but it

57

could not be otherwise; that there was no escape for you; that you could never become a different man; that even if time and faith were still left you to change into something different, you would most likely not wish to change; or if you did wish to, even then you would do nothing; because perhaps in reality there was nothing for you to change into.

This is no forlorn confession; this voice, potent in its estrangement, has passed into a full flowering of its secret being.

The Stunted Self

Thus far we've dealt with the divided self as a special case, advanced in his awareness of the negative, steeped in misanthropy, occupying a world both alien and uninviting. Is it possible that the authors we've read are simply transcribing their own experiences? A glance at the back of the book will tell you that at least one of them is, but that's not really important. More to the point is the seeming accord, in all three passages, of author and voice. We know, from Dr. Johnson's presumptions about the comic romance, that confusing characters with their authors can be a mistake. But the ironic distance the realists imposed between themselves and their creations, overlooked by the Doctor, is missing from these selections.

Let's assume—what is always safest to assume, even in a work of professed nonfiction—that all three passages are wholly invented. Why, if one is an inventor, exalt a patently damaged character into a hero? Presumably for reasons of craft. The author may doubt the willingness of readers to sympathize with an anguished oddball unless his bleak perspective is leavened with wit, humor, and insight—comic relief; or he may have found that portraying a character who *himself* is an inventor—of a secret self, with its own argosy of irony and iconoclasm, its rival vision—so strains his resources that the further exploit of mocking him exceeds his talent.

In any case these authors make clear that the character who nurtures a secret self must have considerable gifts of his own. We can appreciate just what's involved in the enterprise by turning to characters who, for different reasons, fail in the effort. The young man in the next passage is so besieged that he requires a mediating voice, a neutral narrator, to articulate his anguish, and even that mediator can only quietly record the protagonist's moment of crisis, leaving us to guess at its origin and meaning:

On the sub-main floor of the hotel, which the management directed bathers to use, a woman with zinc salve on her nose got into the elevator with the young man.

"I see you're looking at my feet," he said to her when the car was in motion.

"I beg your pardon?" said the woman.

"I said I see you're looking at my feet."

"I *beg* your pardon. I happened to be looking at the floor," said the woman, and faced the doors of the car.

"If you want to look at my feet, say so," said the young man. "But don't be a God-damned sneak about it."

"Let me out of here, please," the woman said quickly to the girl operating the car.

The car doors opened and the woman got out without looking back.

"I have two normal feet and I can't see the slightest God-damned reason why anybody should stare at them," said the young man.

This brief scene radiates estrangement: there is the disquieting repetition of "feet"; the absurdity of "zinc salve" on the woman's nose; and the claustrophic elevator, with its silent operator. The incident seems the result of a small misunderstanding, but only marginally. Under any circumstances an encounter between this pair would leave both wincing. Why does the young man enlist our sympathy? Clearly he's in the wrong. We can well imagine the woman's defense: "He started it. Oh, maybe I *glanced* at his feet, but only for a second, and what of it? You're on the elevator with a stranger, your eyes wander. You fill the time. Besides, what's so special about his feet? They're *his* hangup, not mine." The facts, as lawyers say, are in her favor. The young man *does* start it. His accusation greets her the instant she steps into view, and she responds just as she ought, exiting at the first opportunity, without looking back. She acts as the social principle requires. Yet because his pain is so great, because he has been shaken to the core of his being, we feel for the young man. His final question, uttered after his antagonist departs, is directed not at her, nor at the elevator girl, but at the invisible forces which rule his grief. He hasn't learned to accept the casual violations our privacy must endure everyday. For this we admire him, from our fallen state.

The young man might have a chance if only he possessed a secret self. Obviously he doesn't; instead of assessing his humiliation in a private dream or soliloquy he bares it publicly. His outburst only adds to the pressure building within. It is released in a most final and drastic way when, in his hotel room, he puts a bullet through his head. The dilemma of the divided self is no mere abstraction, but a war, and any skirmish can prove decisive.

The secret self may be inhibited by a deficiency originating not in the personality of the divided self but in the larger conditions of society, as in the following passage:

She would . . . go up to her bedroom, and sit. . . . She ought to be thinking about her life, about herself. But she did not. Or perhaps she could not. As soon

61

as she forced her mind to think about Susan [Rawlings] (for what else did she want to be alone for?), it skipped off to thoughts of butter or school clothes. Or it thought of Mrs. Parkes. She realised that she sat listening for the movements of the cleaning woman, following her every turn, bend, thought. She followed her in her mind from kitchen to bathroom, from table to oven, and it was as if the duster, the cleaning cloth, the saucepan, were in her own hand. She would hear herself saying: No, not like that, don't put that there.... Yet she did not give a damn what Mrs. Parkes did, or if she did it at all. Yet she could not prevent herself from being conscious of her, every minute. Yes, this was what was wrong with her: she needed, when she was alone, to be really alone, with no one near. She could not endure the knowledge that in ten minutes or in half an hour Mrs. Parkes would call up the stairs: "Mrs. Rawlings, there's no silver polish. Madam, we're out of flour."

Susan Rawlings is as trapped as the young man on the elevator. Retreating to her room, she can't withdraw into herself. Downstairs is the cleaning woman, bustling from task to task, reminding her of her proper role. Susan possesses, potentially, a self of her own, responsible to no one; we sense it stirring when we're told she "did not give a damn what Mrs. Parkes did, or if she did it at all," and we cheer. But obligations shut the lid on it. Still, in its brief awakening, it leads her to an important discovery: "she needed, when she was alone, to be really alone, with no one near." She learns she must cultivate a secret self.

Learning and doing are not the same. And there

are imposing obstacles in Susan's path. For one, she's missing her most important ally, her own mind. We're told "it skipped off to thoughts of butter or school clothes. Or it thought of Mrs. Parkes." *It*: an alien object. Of what use to her are her own thoughts when she has no control over them? Hitting upon what's "wrong" with herself is only the first step. She has far to go before she can confidently stave off the claims of others and is taught this the hard way when she tries to make her husband understand her quandary:

"But Susan [he replies], what sort of freedom can you possibly want—short of being dead! Am I ever free? I go to the office, and I have to be there at ten—all right, half past ten, sometimes. And I have to do this or that, don't I? Then I've got to come home at a certain time—I don't mean it, you know I don't—but if I'm not going to be back home at six I telephone you. When can I ever say to myself: I have nothing to be responsible for in the next six hours?"

His argument, Susan admits, is a good one. His situation *is* the same. But "... why did he not feel bound? Why didn't he chafe and become restless? No, there was something really wrong with her and this proved it." One wants, at this point, to grab Susan and shake some sense into her. "Don't you see you're not like him? Of course he doesn't 'chafe and become restless.' He's not a divided self; he's just an over-burdened, underappreciated citizen, and typically indignant about it. If he could make an eleven-o'clock appearance at the office, and drag himself home after six without phoning—if only he could bend the rules a bit—the 'Generalised Life' would suit him fine. But *you're* on the verge of illumination; you've found out something big. All that's 'really wrong' with you is your certainty that you're at fault." The young man on the elevator at least vented his outrage. Susan mutely sinks into catalepsy. Her husband gets one thing right about her: her only hope of freedom is "being dead."

What explains the starved condition of the secret Susan Rawlings? Why hasn't her secret self flourished in the dark? Certainly not for want of trying. At every stage of her doomed progress she stiffens her spine against defeat, grasping for inner equilibrium. She simply hasn't the resources to right herself, nor any idea how to acquire them. Another woman with a room of her own once wrote:

> The most transient visitor to this planet...who picked up this [news]paper could not fail to be aware, even from this scattered testimony, that England is under the rule of a patriarchy....[To man belonged] the power and the money and the influence. He was the proprietor of the paper and its editor and sub-editor. He was the Foreign Secretary and the Judge. He was the cricketer; he owned the racehorses and the yachts. He was the director of the company that pays two hundred per cent to its shareholders. He left millions to charities and colleges that were ruled by himself.

This passage, taken in conjunction with the trials of Susan Rawlings, leads us to a curious place. It now seems that in order to stand against the "Generalised

Life" one must be invited to join it. One must have opportunities for success, prestige, power, personal happiness—the rewards, in short, of the bourgeois journey. But haven't we learned that inhospitable environments are fine soil for the secret self? Take Voice A, the deposed king, or B, the fantasying diarist, or—best of all—the voice from underground. Their perception of the social life as nightmare nourishes, rather than retards, their secret selves. By rights Susan should succeed more spectacularly than those others; she doesn't just think her social burden is oppressive: she can prove it. She's a woman in a patriarchy, enduring its condescending smiles and sly winks. Custom, habit, in some instances recorded law, proclaim her a second-class citizen. The public life discommodes her in most respects, but it ought to provide a perfect foil for the secret self.

Yet she can't begin to nurture it. Culture, in its ultimate offense, has deprived her of her mind. She can't invent a rival world—all her tools have been co-opted in the cause of her own submission. We read how Susan "followed [Mrs. Parkes] in her mind from kitchen to bathroom"; in no part of her being can she follow her impulses, root them out, examine them. For this is what the secret self does. It converts feelings—impressions and sensations—into an alternative vision to be set against the strident claims of the "Generalised Life." It remakes yearnings into a principle of survival on one's own private terms. But Susan is unequipped for such a project; she has only a cavity where a secret self might be.

A Triumphant
Stand-off

The "successfully" divided self, the one who can't go on but goes on, must himself be a kind of artist. Is it possible that the artist must be a divided self? Certainly authors have long empathized with misanthropic characters, more than is demanded by the tenets of craft. Chaucer's Pardoner, Shakespeare's Iago, Milton's Satan, Byron's Don Juan, Conrad's Kurtz, Nabokov's Humbert Humbert; Dostoevsky spawned a whole race of them. As for the misanthropic voice or persona: we hear it in the Old Testament, in the histories and satires of ancient Rome, not to mention modern literary generations disgusted by the "Generalised Life," such as the French Existentialists, most famously Sartre, who rose out of the ashes of World War II, and Italy's Neorealists. Without its powerful hatred for the "Generalised Life" American literature would never have exerted the influence it has in the last hundred and fifty years. Our major writers—from Hawthorne and Poe and Melville to Nathanael West and Norman Mailer—so revile national habits that for many readers their works constitute a rival history of the vaunted American Dream.

What distinguishes them from mere sensationalists is the dimension in their work which I've called psychological. Instead of graphically depicting society at its ghastliest or sliding into indignant rhetoric, they ponder the origins and consequences of their own abhorrence. The psychologist does not settle for saying "X is terrible." He says, "I am repulsed by X," and further, "If I find X repulsive he must matter to me. To be repulsed by him is to be repulsed by a part of myself."

The psychological writer, like the divided self, becomes his own witness; he dotes on himself, not only on his defeats, but on his triumphs:

> My dinner, dress, associates, looks, compliments, dues,
> The real or fancied indifference of some man or woman
>   I love,
> The sickness of one of my folks or of myself, or ill-
>   doing or loss or lack of money, or depressions or
>   exaltations,
> Battles, the horrors of fratricidal war, the fever of
>   doubtful news, the fitful events;
> These come to me days and nights and go from me
>   again,
> But they are not the Me myself.
>
> Apart from the pulling and hauling stands what I
>   am,
> Stands amused, complacent, compassionating, idle,
>   unitary,
> Looks down, is erect, or bends an arm on an
>   impalpable certain rest,

Looking with side-curved head curious what will come
        next,
Both in and out of the game and watching and
        wondering at it....
I believe in you my soul, the other I am must not
        abase itself to you,
And you must not be abased to the other.

Here, in this marvelous, casual-seeming language, are the issues of the chapter laid out as freshly as flowers. First comes a catalogue of public concerns the self must acknowledge, including the mundane (dinner and dress); the painful (illness, unrequited love); and psychic extremes (those "depressions and exaltations" we've been mulling at length). For good measure the poet even adds some truly cataclysmic events, on the world-historical scale, "the horrors of fratricidal war," so we know he's got an ear tuned to the greater discords. Like the other voices, he can't completely escape the "Generalised Life." It "come[s] to me days and nights and go[es] from me again." And, as we would expect, this poet draws a clear line between it and "the Me myself."

But instead of feeling threatened or minimized by "this pulling and hauling," the poet "stands amused, complacent, compassionating, idle, unitary," proclaiming amity where we've grown to expect bitterness or malevolence or suspicion. And that final "unitary" frankly mocks the condition of inner dividedness. What we would predict his secret self—"the Me myself"— to oppose, it accepts, without irony or paradox. So strong is "the Me myself" that it loiters willingly on the margin of the "Generalised Life," "compassion-ating."

Can it be that he is too thick to reckon the cost of involvement? Not when we see how thoroughly versed he is in the dilemma of the divided self. He formulates it in language as explicit as Hamlet's "to be or not to be":

> I believe in you my soul, the other I am must not
> abase itself to you,
> And you must not be abased to the other.

This poet has somehow achieved the belief that both his selves, public and private, are solely his. He's not divided so much as doubled, an achievement of almost unimaginable egoism, like swallowing the creation whole. But we know the achievement has been suffered for. "Abase[ment]" suggests a prior experience of humiliation that can never be rubbed from memory.

VOICES OF PROPHECY: VISIONARY LITERATURE

"The ancient bottoms of the sea have become mountain ridges."

—*LEONARDO DA VINCI*

The Visionary Faculty

As we've moved from passage to passage the distance between author and invention has narrowed. The first authors in "Things as They Are," no less than their characters "drawn from the living world," were impersonators, their mimicries indexes of confident objectivity. In subsequent selections this confidence faltered: inventor and invented were joined in bafflement before the elusive surfaces of reality. "Myself Am Hell" added a new twist, voices so authoritative in their contempt for the "Generalised Life" that they seemed to reflect the submerged opinions of their creators. Soon it became difficult to know who was actually addressing us. Surely in the last passage the distinction was erased: poet and "I" converged.

In this chapter the accord between author and voice is complete. This does not mean they are, in every case, identical—we'll encounter fabricated "I"s—but that the words on the page are a window to the author's own struggle to fit perceptions into language and thus carry a greater burden than they did for the realist or the psychologist. They too had to master language, of course; but their projects were different. The realist was interested in mirroring the prevailing rhythms of the public life. We had something concrete to gauge his invention against: our own experience. The psychologist plumbs concealed conflicts; his method, though, is to present the outward and recognizable features of distress—the speech and gestures and actions of the alienated, measurable against experiences of our own. Nonetheless the psychologist's skill at sounding the deep currents of the mind approximates an even rarer gift, the visionary faculty, which discloses and vivifies the unknowable.

Visionary writing is concerned with revelation. For this reason it is often confused with mysticism. But there is a crucial difference. The mystic's discoveries come to him as sudden beams from above; he has a pipeline to the Infinite. The visionary, by contrast, hews a trail to illumination marked for others to follow.

Before looking at some classic visionary writing, we should get a clearer idea of what the visionary author assays. The following two passages can be called visionary experiments—that is, they try to formulate new ways of thinking about an experience.

(1)

After three days of waiting [on the island] for the sight of some human face, Decoud caught himself entertaining a doubt of his own individuality. It had merged into the world of cloud and water, of natural forces and forms of nature. In our activity alone do we find the sustaining illusion of an independent existence as against the whole scheme of things of which we form a helpless part.

_____

(2)

"According to nature" you want to *live*? O you noble Stoics, what deceptive words these are! Imagine a being like nature, wasteful beyond measure, indifferent beyond measure, without purposes and consideration, without mercy and justice, fertile and desolate and uncertain at the same time; imagine indifference itself as a power—how *could* you live according to this indifference? Living—is that not precisely wanting to be other than this nature? Is not living—estimating, preferring, being unjust, being limited, wanting to be different? And supposing your imperative "live according to nature" meant at bottom as much as "live according to life"— how could you *not* do that? Why make a principle of what you yourselves are and must be?

In truth, the matter is altogether different: while you pretend rapturously to read the canon of your law in nature, you want something opposite, you strange actors and self-deceivers! Your pride wants to impose your mortality, your ideal, on nature— even on nature—and incorporate them in her....

Both authors are at pains to demonstrate that nature opposes what is heroic in us. Nothing fancy so far: who hasn't seen "Man against Nature" chalked on the blackboard (just below "Man against Society" and "Man against Himself")? Here, however, the usual proposition is altered. What makes nature opponent to man

in these passages is not its imperiousness but its ignobility; nature degrades him. The first passage describes
a devouring "world of cloud and water, of natural
forces and forms;" the second equates the laws of
nature with a litany of base human attributes.

Let's begin with the first, which we may paraphrase
as follows: Decoud, having forfeited his human identity, dependent on the presence of others, undergoes
a spiritual death that reduces him to an element of
nature, like cloud and water. To vivify this occurrence,
and convey its magnitude, the author suggests a polar-
ity between the human and the natural through the
concept of the one versus the many: Decoud and "some
human face" signify the one (human "individuality");
"the world of cloud and water, of natural forces and
forms of nature" signifies the many (nature). The
problem with this arrangement is that one versus many
doesn't suggest repellent or polar opposition; as equal
halves of a single concept, they are, instead, inter-
dependent, like two sides of an equation. The first
clue that something is amiss is the verb "merge": its
image is not precisely one of essential alteration (*A*
transformed into *B*), but of a small thing absorbed
into an aggregation of like things, as a rill merges into
a stream, or a face into a crowd. The secondary meanings of "forms" (bodies, as in human bodies) and
"forces" (a cohesive group, e.g., "armed forces") but-
tress this notion of homogeneity. Thus, as the author
openly confesses, Decoud doesn't change into an element of nature; he never was anything but. Such a
design, with its "forms," "forces," and "scheme," is

heavily indebted to medieval "proofs" of the existence of God, and leaves us not with a dramatization but with an age-old rationalization. This is confirmed by the last sentence's rhetorical flourish, wherein detachment suddenly gives way to confession; the author is not describing Decoud's plight but his own—it is he who has failed to sustain an illusion; his sentences, for all their beauty, falter before the occult truth they're meant to evoke, and succeed only in naming it. And in this instance naming is a kind of avoidance.

Author No. 2 is equally tricky. After one sentence he's got us by the lapels (the second-person address is a good technique). And he does a stellar job of demystifying nature. (Every reader must be persuaded by his argument that imputing ideals to nature is mistaken and self-glorifying.) But he's snared, as was the first author, in abstractions—for instance, "indifference" and "power." When he says, "Is not living ... wanting to be different," we're reminded of the first passage, with its "activity" providing a "sustaining illusion." This author has much to teach us about ourselves and how we distort nature, but he doesn't show nature in a new light.

Here is one final attempt to make nature "other":

> As for the grass, it grew as scant as hair
> In leprosy; thin dry blades pricked the mud
> Which underneath looked kneaded up with blood.

This, at a glance, seems the weakest candidate of all. The landscape described is manifestly, almost painfully, human, its muddy ground a leprous scalp, its few sickly blades of grass like hair. The image is of a diseased carcass. Still, we must concede that, unlike the first author, this poet strips nature of any connection to the divine. He follows the second in assigning nature unpleasant traits, although where the second author spoke of moral qualities—nature is wasteful, indifferent, cruel, a malign intelligence—these few lines offer no discernible intelligence to match our wits against, only that most familiar yet alien landscape, the human body. The poet's image shocks us into discovering that the victorious opponent of our "individuality" and "pride" is, in the end, the husk that houses them.

Images, not formulations, lead us to perceptual insight. We saw this in the passage from Homer, where Odysseus used metaphors to give a sensible reading of nature. I went on to say that for the writer metaphorical readings don't come easily since he, like the rest of us, brings an analytical bias to language: it no longer seems a vast storehouse of names and myths but a highly ordered system.* The result is that the visionary, who's interested neither in things as they

---

*It always *was* a system, in Homer's time and before. Psychologists argue that language is a specialized mental operation—there may in fact be a "language organ" located in the brain—of such inherent complexity that it is ridiculous even to differentiate between primitive and advanced linguistic uses. Our interest, of course, is in one specific kind of language, literary discourse, which, as it faces a growing and complicating world, must refurbish itself. Thus the need for "new" metaphors to describe experiences unknown in times past and therefore lacking adequate names.

are nor in things hidden, but in things as they might be if seen with heightened powers of perception, must make startling imaginative leaps which prose, descended from the logical tradition of ideas in sequence, scarcely encourages.

Vision as Myth

We have seen one kind of vision. It defamiliarized nature through strong and unusual images. The following comes from a medieval poet's imagination of hell. Originally written in three-line stanzas, it appears here in a prose translation:

> While I kept my eyes on [the thieves], lo, a serpent with six feet darts up in front of one and fastens on him all over; with the middle feet it clasped the paunch and with those in front seized the arms, then set its fangs in the one cheek and the other; the hind feet it spread on the thighs and thrust its tail between them and stretched it up over the loins behind. Never was ivy so rooted to a tree as the horrid beast intertwined the other's members with its own; then, as if they had been of hot wax, they stuck together and mixed their colours and

neither the one nor the other appeared now what it was before; thus spreads over the paper before the flame a dark colour that is not yet black, and the white dies off. The other two [thieves] were looking on and each cried: 'O me, Agnello, how thou changest! Lo, thou art now neither two nor one!' Now the two heads had become one, when the two shapes appeared to us blended in one face in which the two were lost; two arms were made of the four lengths; the thighs with the legs, the belly and the chest, became such members as were never seen. Each former feature was blotted out; the perverted shape seemed both and neither, and such, with slow pace, it moved away.

This vision shows an unlikely event in as matter-of-fact a light as possible. Thus its three similes, each visual, belong to the realm of everyday observation: (1) ivy hugging a tree; (2) melting wax; and (3) paper held over a flame. Were the scene not so obviously invented, we might suspect the poet of a taste for the pornographic; his effects depend on a similarly detached hyperrealism. The acuteness of description—"the two arms were made of the four lengths; the thighs with the legs, the belly and the chest"—is both riveting and distressing. The actual pornographer, of course, details ordinary aggressiveness, thereby plugging into experiences already known to the reader. In this passage the poet uses our gullibility for authoritative depiction to make a mythical transformation seem vivid. In the instant we recoil we are convinced.

Phantasmal serpents, images of fire and heat—we

might never expect them to be so graphically presented, but since they intimately figure in the mythology of Christianity we are, in a sense, prepared to accept them. This next passage has only a slanting reference to recognizable myths:

> Los was the fourth immortal starry one, & in the
> Earth
> Of a bright Universe Empery attended day & night
> Days & nights of revolving joy, Urthona was his
> name
> In Eden; in the Auricular Nerves of Human life
> Which is the Earth of Eden, he his Emanations
> propagated
> Fairies of Albion afterwards Gods of the Heathen,
> Daughter of Beulah
> Sing
> His fall into Division & his Resurrection to Unity
> His fall into the Generation of Decay & Death &
> his Regeneration
> by the Resurrection from the dead . . .

If the reader had doubts about the singularity of visionary literature, they should now be dispelled. Here is an author with his own way of looking at things, and the things themselves are elusive. What, for instance, are the "Auricular Nerves of Human Life"? "Auricular" has to do with ears; auricular nerves must be the physiological equipment that enables us to hear. What makes them synonymous with the "Earth of Eden"? Perhaps the hearing sense, representing undiluted perception, refers to the harmonious relation to nature we enjoyed in our Edenic past. Odysseus, we remember, was bound to nature by his pure perception of it. If we further suppose "auricular" to contain a pun on "oracular," the poet's phrase takes on a prophetic meaning: to perceive the world through imagination is to decipher its deep mysteries, its occult operations.

As Eden is but a memory or wish, so must be the undiluted powers of his auricular nerves—imagination and prophecy don't visit beings who have fallen into "Division" and "the Generation of Decay & Death." "Division" resembles the inner dividedness discussed in "Myself Am Hell," the self reduced to warring factions. Before he can retrieve his ancient innocence Los must be restored to interior "Unity," and from the depths of "the Generation of Decay & Death" achieve "Regeneration," spiritual health. These lines, then, are the prelude to an updated account of the most familiar story in the Western world, the biblical fall and redemption of Man. Los begins happily in Eden, then is bedeviled by sin. Finally, following the example of Christ, he is resurrected.

What makes the passage difficult is its idiosyncratic language. Words here don't have the meanings we're used to. This poet's phrases are like the mysteries he's pledged to explain. If language is the visionary's lone vehicle for communication, why use words that defy quick understanding? Perhaps the poet doesn't want to be understood too quickly, if understanding only leads us someplace we've already been. Up to now we have regarded words as impartial and flexible. But is this assumption tenable? Isn't every word imprinted with meanings decreed by culture? The visionary, especially in an epoch which favors analysis over intuition, may fear that conventional language has become a barrier to understanding. He can retreat into silence, which seems an admission of defeat, or he can try to wrench words from the iron jaws of approved usage, putting them to uses of his own. Here he risks losing those readers who demand familiar language; but such readers may well be immune to insight, no matter how clearly it's expressed.

Foretellings of Doom

The visionary's interpretive gifts come most obviously into play when he addresses the future. We all revere those savants who in the comfortably distant past gazed serenely into a crystal ball and predicted some startling feature of the present, like television or brain surgery. A famous example is Da Vinci, with his sketches of flying machines, or Tocqueville, whose *Democracy in America* predicted a hundred and fifty years ago the hegemony of the United States and Russia. What pleases us about such foretellings is that they quietly approve what we have become, confirm-

ing us as children of destiny. But the literary visionary
is clairvoyant in a different way. His glimpses into the
future tend to be dire, not only because they yield
disastrous possibilities, but because the moment of
insight is not something we are ever really prepared
for. Most literature, like most lives, is predicated on
continuity—comprehensible beginnings, middles, and
ends. The visitation of sudden insight can be terri-
fying:

> Howl ye; for the day of the Lord is at hand; it shall
> come as a destruction from the Almighty. There-
> fore shall all hands be faint, and every man's heart
> shall melt: And they shall be afraid: pangs and
> sorrows shall take hold of them; they shall be in
> pain as a woman that travaileth; they shall be amazed
> one at another; their faces shall be as flames. Behold,
> the day of the Lord cometh, cruel both with wrath
> and fierce anger, to lay the land desolate: and he
> shall destroy the sinners thereof out of it. For the
> stars of heaven and the constellations thereof shall
> not give their light: the sun shall be darkened in
> his going forth, and the moon shall not cause her
> light to shine. And I will punish the world for their
> evil, and the wicked for their iniquity; and I will
> cause the arrogancy of the proud to cease, and will
> lay low the haughtiness of the terrible. I will make
> a man more precious than fine gold; even a man
> than the golden wedge of Ophir. Therefore I will
> shake the heavens, and the earth shall remove out
> of her place, in the wrath of the Lord of hosts, and
> in the day of his fierce anger.

This grand prophecy enfolds the entire universe,
though its claims—that sun and moon will turn cold,

stars blink out like city lights—strain our credulity, rather as the serpent in hell did. As we shrank from that image we conferred on it a kind of possibility; this vision grips us by postulating an instant of wholesale destruction which, fanciful as it seems, coheres into a web of tightly linked images exploiting the manifold associations of fire. There is the fire of heat ("and every man's heart shall melt"); flame ("their faces shall be as flames"); ashes ("lay the land desolate"); light ("the constellations thereof shall not give their light"); the forge ("the golden wedge of Ophir"). The temporal progression of these images is circular, from life to death to resurrection. The spatial route the blaze travels is linear and upward: from the ground it climbs up through the body to the face, moves outward to consume the landscape, shoots vertically into the sky, and finally reaches the galaxy—a ladder linking heart to heaven.

About imminent dangers, we're told plenty by this prediction: whatever is, won't be. Of subsequent developments we learn only that a new man will be beamed down among the ashes, evidently to begin the process anew. The rule with apocalyptic visions is that the moment of ruin is presented more persuasively than the aftermath. The visionary claims to see things in their ultimate clarity, with an absolute intensity of perception. When he foretells disaster he's really unmasking the secret of the present. Isaiah's prophecy is less a warning than a rebuke: we don't think, I'd better find a bunker one of these days. We think, Time to mend my ways.

When his eyes lift toward the future, the visionary can lose his bearings. The following prophetic poem, one of the most famous in our language, was written in the early part of this century. It contains two movements: the first, as in Isaiah, describes the moment of ruin as a current event; the second ventures to describe what must come of it:

> Turning and turning in the widening gyre
> The falcon cannot hear the falconer;
> Things fall apart; the centre cannot hold;
> Mere anarchy is loosed upon the world,
> The blood-dimmed tide is loosed, and everywhere
> The ceremony of innocence is drowned;
> The best lack all conviction, while the worst
> Are full of passionate intensity.
>
> Surely some revelation is at hand;
> Surely the Second Coming is at hand.
> The Second Coming! Hardly are those words out
> When a vast image out of Spiritus Mundi
> Troubles my sight: somewhere in sands of the desert
> A shape with lion body and the head of a man,
> A gaze blank and pitiless as the sun,
> Is moving its slow thighs, while all about it
> Reel shadows of the indignant desert birds.
> The darkness drops again; but now I know
> That twenty centuries of stony sleep
> Were vexed to nightmare by a rocking cradle,
> And what rough beast, its hour come round at last,
> Slouches towards Bethlehem to be born?

Let's begin with the first part. Does it state a general principle or announce, in the present tense of a newspaper headline, a specific occurrence? Perhaps both.

It is the tendency of "things" to "fall apart"; and "things," as the poet speaks, are collapsing. And what are "things"? The plainest word in the language, its meaning here is cryptic indeed. Since their collapse presages anarchy, things may be civilizations. Not a single civilization, but all of them, anarchy having been "loosed upon the world."

Instead of the Bible's fire, this poem features an element equally capable of destruction—water. Anarchy sweeps in a "tide" that seems, again, both general and specific. Generally, insurrections travel in waves from nation to nation (think of Europe in the nineteenth century, or Central America in the twentieth). In the specific terms of the lyric's imagery, blood spills into water and is borne from border to border, "drown[ing]" at each stop the "ceremony of innocence."

"Ceremony of innocence": a troublesome, though lovely, phrase. Webster's string of definitions for "ceremony" concludes with this: "observance of an established code of civility or politeness." Civility or politeness—nice manners? Are they all that's at stake here? Not quite. The Oxford English Dictionary tells us that "civility" is "connected with citizenship and civil polity." The drowning of polity—political organization—*that* sounds like anarchy. What about "politeness": how does it figure in this catastrophic loss? It refers to personal relations, the "delicious old-fashioned Values" whose decline Moses Herzog mourns. Thus ceremony involves respect for both political and personal codes.

Why ceremony "of innocence"? What kind of ceremony does innocence perform? We note first that "innocence" has many applications; there's innocence from crime, from sin, from experience, from knowledge. As a state of being we often associate it with childhood: we are said in our early years to live *in* innocence, a mythical place, like Eden. Ceremony, with its "established codes," seems the reverse of innocence. It implies initiation, sheddings of innocence, from religious rites to civic duties to activities combining both—weddings, say, and funerals. Ceremonies in this sense mark the end of innocence. Yet they also depend on it. Rituals and initiations, after all, are highly symbolic—the bride wears white, the corpse a smile; prayers are intoned, heads bowed. None of it means anything without the participants' deep-seated belief and trust. Innocence hallows ceremony.

The second part of the vision introduces the biblical promise of redemption, though the "Second Coming" depicted here is no "man more precious than gold" but a horrific creature ("A shape with lion body and the head of a man, A gaze blank and pitiless as the sun")—the Messiah translated into a Darwinian hypothesis, as though the poet were saying, "Let's suppose there *is* a second coming, the arrival of a specimen projected from our canniest imaginings. What sort of being will he be?" A cross between the animal ("lion body"), the human ("head of a man"), and the elemental (its gaze "blank and pitiless as the sun"); a monster, hideously alien, yet familiar—the image is of a sphinx. Sphinxes pose riddles. Does the second coming portend sheer disaster, or does it hold out hope? "Twenty centuries" of antiquity trembled before the birth of Christ, in his "rocking cradle." Some would claim that he was Isaiah's "man more precious than gold." What ensues after the version of civilized life he fostered collapses into dust? It is a riddle even the visionary can't answer.

Reality Intrudes

Before the horrid serpent, the "generation of decay," the earth yanked out of orbit, the "blood-dimmed tide," stands the poet, witness with his heightened powers to the unimaginable, sending up a cry of amazement. But once his words reach our ears what are we supposed to do? How are we to resurrect ourselves into Unity, or grow less wicked, or take arms against waves of anarchy? When measured against the visionary's project of reform, the political program with its agenda of "attainable goals," its "realistic expectations," seems slight and bland, an embarrassment to human possibility. More money here, less there, shuffled "priorities." Yet when such thin changes are wrought we are impressed, and with good reason. For the most part the human community, in all its collective endeavors, just muddles along. Our greatest triumph is usually *not* doing, keeping things in balance, refraining from the act we can't redeem. The visionary operates within this knowledge; he urges action, but an action of seeing. To see as if we'd never before had eyes, as if our works were wholly new to us, unnamed; to recover the ancient power of inventing the world in the instant we look hard at it—this is the visionary project. The poem itself, no less than what it describes, is the vision.

For all its verbal extravagance, visionary literature discerns the hidden configurations of visible things, and thus oddly resembles realism. Their affinities are patent. Both are interested in discovery; both are developmental, describing a progression from one state of awareness to another; both turn on surprise and recognition, crucial moments when things seem not at all what we imagined; both, finally, refer the reader back to himself and his habits of seeing. The differences are also apparent. In realism the reigning sense is of continuity. We are left with a hero, bruised and wise, who has learned a lesson. Life proceeds in its accustomed rhythms; rituals and polity impose order on society. The copier of human manners plants himself in the middle of experience and, for all the linear progress he chronicles—from youth to age, misreading to understanding, poverty to wealth (and, perhaps, poverty again)—*arrives* in the middle. Future and past extend into the horizon. Visionary literature,

90

on the other hand, has an air of finality; it addresses the pulse point of crisis; humanity and nature are tensed for the consummation of flame or tide. Progress is thus discontinuous, one state of being abruptly veering into another. Not, as the mystic has it, because insight is bestowed on us, but because our capacity for imaginative apprehension, inwardly cultivated, leads us past the outposts of knowledge.

Imagine a place where these two paths to enlightenment cross, where visionary insight takes on the guise of a lesson occurring within the context of continuity, and the realistic lesson, the discovery of things as they are, constitutes a sudden veering toward insight. The following poem is a translation from the French by Robert Lowell:

> While I was walking in a pitted place,
> crying aloud against the human race,
> letting thoughts ramble here and there apart—
> knives singing on the whetstone of my heart—
> I saw a cloud descending on my head
> in the full noon, a cloud inhabited
> by black devils, sharp, humped, inquisitive
> as dwarfs. They knew where I was sensitive,
> now idling there, and looked me up and down,
> as cool delinquents watch a madman clown.
> I heard them laugh and snicker blasphemies,
> while swapping signs and blinking with their eyes.
>
> "Let's stop and watch this creature at our leisure—
> all sighs and sweaty hair. We'll take his measure.
> It's a great pity that this mountebank
> and ghost of Hamlet strutting on a plank

> should think he's such an artist at his role
> he has to rip the lining from his soul
> and paralyze the butterflies and bees
> with a peepshow of his indecencies—
> and even we, who gave him his education,
> must listen to his schoolboy declamation."
>
> Wishing to play a part (my pride was high
> above the mountains and the devil's cry)
> like Hamlet now, I would have turned my back,
> had I not seen among the filthy pack
> (Oh crime that should have made the sun drop dead!)
> my heart's queen and the mistress of my bed
> there purring with the rest at my distress,
> and sometimes tossing them a stale caress.

This poem, like the last, consists of two parts—actually, as we'll see, two visions. Again, we'll take them in order. First, the "black devils." Although spawned by the poet's fancy, they appear to him as reality. A small verb does the trick. The poet says, "I *saw* a cloud descending on my head." Ordinarily when we refer to a change of mood—as this poet is doing—we speak of our feelings. We "feel" a cloud descending. Yet this poet not only *sees* a change overtake him, he sees it in a place the eyes seldom search: directly above his head. This suggests his sight (his *vision*) is better than yours and mine. In the space of a few lines he has slipped out of his skin and climbed to some aerial height from which he peers down at the top of his own skull.

Such objectivity recalls the scrupulous delineation of the serpent we read earlier in this chapter. There are further resemblances. Here too are vivid details, and the slow-motion intensity of a nightmare. And just as the multi-limbed beast seemed palpable, these black devils, "sharp, humped, inquisitive as dwarfs," boldly accost the eye. In one respect this poet outdoes the poet of hell: he endows his inventions with personality. "They knew where I was sensitive," he tells us bitterly; they look him "up and down/...laugh and snicker blasphemies, while swapping signs and blinking with their eyes." The concluding simile of the first verse paragraph might be taken from "actual life." The reader has probably witnessed the spectacle of a madman raving while adolescents, "cool delinquents," egg him on. The devils are becoming more credible than the poet. Not they, but he, seems freakish and unreal.

The second paragraph completes the reversal. In ten lines of direct quotation, the devils jeer in concert at their creator, and they make a good case: the poet is a poseur, a fake Hamlet who "has to rip the lining from his soul/and paralyze the butterflies and bees/with a peepshow of his indecencies." He is, in short, an exhibitionist. Or, rather, would be: the street is empty, no one is watching. What are we to make of a man who, with such dedication to realism, invents the scene of his own degradation, whose fantasy doesn't, like the improvisations of "Myself Am Hell," provide him with the solitude needed by his secret self, but accomplishes the opposite, populating his thoughts with others? A useful vision, this seems suspiciously restorative, a trifle trumped-up.

But the poem doesn't end on a note of chastisement. Just as the rigged episode concludes there occurs a rude twist, a bruising glimpse of the poet's "heart's queen," posing amid the devils as a sort of moll, "purring with the rest at my distress, and sometimes tossing them a stale caress." Here is the true insight for which the encounter with the devils was only a deceptive prelude. The key word is in the last line: "stale" (the French *sale* actually means "dirty" or "soiled") describes not only the lover's caresses but the poet's attempt to clothe a banality in visionary grandeur. Like the sorcerer's apprentice, he has tapped the visionary reservoir and found it's a demonic source, the origin not just of invention, but of discovery.

Since the visionary faculty resists being harnessed, it can arise, like intimations of the "negative," when least desired. Thus any long look at the world or the self may yield insights which leap over the boundaries of text. This chapter has featured verse because its images compress large revelations into a few lines. We could return to the prose passages of the previous chapters and observe the visionary faculty at work. The two selections from Proust dismantle our assumptions about appearance and reality. The paean from underground makes us reconsider our suppositions about the impotence of solitude. And wasn't Susan Rawlings's brave look into the abyss a visionary episode?

It should by now be apparent that our thematic categories are not exclusive. Each describes one facet of the experience of reading. We seldom read only for representation of the "living world." Nor are we satisfied with a view of the depths, important as they are to understanding literature. The visionary insight is probably the most astonishing we ever encounter in a book. But without surfaces and depths, without familiar textures, what meaning would revelations have?

ILLUSION AND INDULGENCE: LITERATURE AS A GAME

"In the increasingly convincing darkness
The words become palpable, like a fruit
That is too beautiful to eat."

—JOHN ASHBERY

The Spirit of Play

Visionary literature presented us for the first time with passages that taxed our powers of interpretation. No longer could we gaze past the clear surface of language to its proliferating undergrowth of intentions and implication. Suddenly the surface itself had clouded over; a small revelatory feat was now involved just in deciphering the overt message. What did "ceremony of innocence" mean? Did it mean all those things? Were we just imputing meanings to it? From such questions flow others, more general and basic: is there a way out of the maze of meanings inscribed in language by tradition and habit? Can we recover the bracing pleasure of seizing words as they come?

Such matters lead us back to the ancient crossroads where sacral singing met the complexities of the sentence, words-as-names being consumed into the process, or system, of language. This development, as we've seen, proved both a drawback and a benefit. The magical union of singer and hearer, assured by live performance, was now lost, only partly compensated by the conceit of the "voice." But language as process had a powerfully redeeming virtue: it enabled the author to interpose a distance between himself and his experience. As a result he examined reality with scrupulous detachment. The ironic viewpoint was born, and with it the notion of realistic, impartial literature. This was liberating. But, like all innovations, it introduced a new set of limitations. For the psychologist and the visionary, realism, with its fixed epicenter of rational values, stood as a barrier to new perception. Exposing the disparity between what seems and what is doesn't help the writer who probes beneath the shell of the "Generalised Life." The psychologist favors unique plangent voices charged with vivacity and wit, or their equally eloquent opposite, voices gone silent or toneless. The visionary gives words new incarnations: "the Auricular Nerves of Human life"; "ceremony of innocence." To ponder them is to ponder the depths of language. By repudiating single, imposed *meanings* they widened the prospects of *meaning*. Can the same be said of this sphinx-like sentence:

For who is there who anything of some significance has apprehended but is conscious that that exterior splendour may be the surface of a downwardtending lutulent reality or on the contrary anyone so is there inilluminated as not to perceive that as no nature's boon can contend against the bounty of increase so it behoves every most just citizen to become the exhortator and admonisher of his semblables and to tremble lest what had in the past been by the nation excellently commenced might be in the future not with similar excellence accomplished if an inverecund habit shall have gradually traduced the honourable by ancestors transmitted customs to that thither of profundity that that one was audacious excessively who would have the hardihood to rise affirming that no more odious offence can for anyone be than to oblivious neglect to consign that evangel simultaneously command and promise which on all mortals with prophecy of abundance or with diminution's menace that exalted of reiteratedly procreating function ever irrevocably enjoined?

The difficulties in the previous chapter bound author and reader in an interpretive adventure. Familiar words took on new life for us, and, as a consequence, the world itself seemed renewed. But with this prose we suspect that even after consulting the dictionary, and piecing together the lunatic syntax, it still won't add up to anything. "Downwardtending lutulent reality," "exhortator and admonisher of his semblables," "reiteratedly procreating function." It's not meanings that are complex here, it's the words themselves. They sound like a put-on.

Of course: a put-on. A long coil of impressive utterances, bulging with polysyllables. High-class doubletalk. It looks significant, so in our addiction to meaning we start digging for the bone. And when we find there is no bone we realize we have been put on not only by the author but—how humiliating!—by ourselves. In an odd and unexpected way words have once again become sounds; we recover a moment of innocence before language. But this is no magic-carpet ride into the heroic age of bards and epics: Where are the stormy seas, the exhaling gods, the sublime straightforwardness? The only thicket here is the thicket of words. The paradox stated in "Song and Sentence," that the author who wishes to recover meaning must duel with "arts and philosophies," has led us to language which seduces us into interpretation only to overload our interpretive circuits. The modern author can't shut his eyes against the specter of meaning. He must outwit it. In the electronic age "sacred night" falls only after the wires melt.

In addition to liberating us from meaning, this passage is prankish. Each of our categories has accommodated some degree of playfulness. Realists delighted in impersonations and mimicry; divided souls like flashing their wit; even visionaries vented a passion for the calculated effect. This outlandish author does them all one better. Look at this rambling idiocy of words, he seems to say, look what I can do with them. Though the obstreperous "I" is in exile, the extreme self-consciousness of his language makes this author more present in his language than the others. His rival world is invented, not from the reassembled fragments of shifting and fluid reality, or from sounded depths, nor even from heightened powers of perception. His world is built of words themselves.

The Stage and
the Put-on

Every author is primarily a prankster, dealing in an advanced form of practical joke. Telescoped incidents pretend to mirror the progress of a life; feature and gesture are welded into a weightless phantasm called a "character"; musical phrases tease us to the edge of an apocalyptic cliff. Such triumphs are not wholly explicable: knowing it's a gimmick doesn't blunt the amazement when the golden coin is plucked from behind one's ear. It is the magical quality in a poem or story, more than its insight or linguistic richness, which makes us think of writers as artists. Magic in its plainest definition: supernatural effects wrought by human means—sorcery or witchcraft.

The literary shaman is especially at home in the theater. What, after all, is a play, any play, but something put on for a crowd of willing takers? Think of all the solid objects at the inventor's disposal. Actors put on makeup and costumes, scenery is put on a bare stage, lights put on the whole spectacle. The result of all this putting on: a bunch of strangers repeating to the letter a formularized charade of intimacy, night after night, for weeks, months, even years, each time pretending they've never done it before. But—when the lights are brought up and the dead man rises and out trots his murderer, both smiling in the warmth of applause rained down by us—are we not the most absurd of all?

Many playwrights, fully attuned to the inherent and delicious unreality of the stage, exploit its patent pretenses, reminding the audience that it's a play up there, on those boards, beneath those lights. Exaggerating the make-believe needn't diminish the experience. The effect can be just the opposite. A tinge of artificiality alerts the theatergoer to the specialness of what he's witnessing, to the fact that it's an event, even if staged and long rehearsed. Thus in the history of theater are many plays within plays. The youthful protagonist of Chekhov's *The Seagull* is himself a fledgling dramatist whose first effort is staged for the other characters and ourselves. In Ionesco's *The Bald Soprano* a family carries on in demented parody of any number of British drawing-room dramas, exchanging bizarre and nonsensical anecdotes, mindlessly conversing in non sequiturs. The main characters in Tom Stoppard's *The Real Inspector Hound* are a pair of critics reviewing the opening of a play, which, as it unfolds before the critics' eyes and our own, takes off on a staple of popular theater, the "whodunit":

MRS. DRUDGE *(into phone):* Hello, the drawing-room of Lady Muldoon's country residence one morning in early spring? ... H*ello!*—the draw—Who? Whom did you wish to speak to? I'm afraid there is no one of that name here, this is all very mysterious and I'm sure it's leading up to something, I hope nothing is amiss for we, that is Lady Muldoon and her house-guests, are here cut off from the world, including Magnus, the wheelchair-ridden half-brother of her ladyship's husband Lord Albert Muldoon who ten years ago went out for a walk on the cliffs and was never seen again.

Put-ons in plays are usually not quite so silly. Usually they lead to key revelations. This is no accident. It is in our artificial moments, our relaxations of vigilance, that we disclose our secrets. Probably the most famous play within a play occurs in *Hamlet*, when the hero employs a troupe of actors in an attempt to wring a murder confession from his mother and the new husband she has taken. Hamlet guesses that the intimacy of performance will unmask them of caution; illusion provides a cover for the truth.

No less princely in his mingling of truth and pretense was the great Victorian playwright Oscar Wilde. In *The Importance of Being Earnest*, the premier drawing-room comedy in English-speaking theater, he put on, with sublime hyperbole, the snobbery and hypocrisy of an entire culture. The intricate plot involves a pair of young gentlemen who assume the sly alias Ernest (a favorite name of the era) as they covertly pursue libertine lives. All of us, Wilde suggests, must be actors to add luster to the bleak roles assigned us by convention. This wonderful play distills the essence

105

of the most preposterous performance of all, "actual life." These are its opening lines:

ALGERNON. Did you hear what I was playing, Lane?

LANE [Algernon's butler]. I didn't think it polite to listen, sir.

ALGERNON. I'm sorry for that, for your sake. I don't play accurately—anyone can play accurately—but I play with wonderful expression. As far as the piano is concerned, sentiment is my forte. I keep science for life.

LANE. Yes, sir.

ALGERNON. And, speaking of the science of life, have you got the cucumber sandwiches cut for Lady Bracknell?

LANE. Yes, sir.

ALGERNON. . . . by the way, Lane, I see from your book that on Thursday night, when Lord Shoreman and Mr. Worthing were dining with me, eight bottles of champagne are entered as having been consumed.

LANE. Yes, sir; eight bottles and a pint.

ALGERNON. Why is it that at a bachelor's establishment the servants invariably drink the champagne? I ask merely for information.

LANE. I attribute it to the superior quality of the wine, sir. I have often observed that in married households the champagne is rarely of a first-rate brand.

ALGERNON. Good Heavens! Is marriage so demoralizing as that?

LANE. I believe it *is* a very pleasant state, sir. I have had very little experience of it myself up to the present. I have only been married once. That was in consequence of a misunderstanding between myself and a young person.

The ultimate madness of class-ordered society is exposed not by its injustices but, rather, by the liberties it encourages. When Lane blandly informs his employer that he has ignored his piano playing, we understand him to be capitalizing on his social inferiority in order to evade an honest opinion. Algernon's equal would be forced to choose between a lie and the truth. And though we laugh at Lane's imperial insouciance about the missing champagne, we observe that the same principle which prohibits "impolite" listening sanctions stealing. The master-servant relationship, predicated on feudal values of obligation and mutual responsibility, has degenerated into a kind of anarchy. And it begins, as anarchy often does, in language. Nietzsche once wrote that in the autumn of civilization, when personal freedom ripens into decadence, words punish more cruelly than blows. Though Wilde's vision is comic he too recognizes the brutal possibilities of language; in his glittering world words are detached from consequences; any riposte is permitted as long as it's well said. In a way Algernon and Lane repudiate meaning as radically as the impenetrable prose we looked at before. *The Importance of Being Earnest*, like a two-nosed Picasso portrait, exhibits such fidelity to the distortions embodied in "actual life" that we feel threadbare in our own lame habits of seeing.

Breaking the Rules

You can't have a put-on without something to put on. What's the use of a joke about whodunits without whodunits, and, further, without an audience that has seen or read them? Nor can you lampoon a non-existent social order. The first passage we looked at, the labyrinthine sentence, put on language itself. Deciphering its phrases was trouble enough (does "the honourable by ancestors transmitted customs" mean "the honourable customs transmitted by ancestors" or "the customs transmitted by honourable ancestors"? does "than to oblivious neglect to consign" mean "than to consign to oblivious neglect" or "than, oblivious, to consign to neglect"); without some knowledge of Latin, whose syntax this skewed phrasing borrows, one misses the jest. To *appreciate* the jest one must have read some old English prose.* The sentence was a parody, and parodies are a kind of in-joke.

*Though not very old; take a look at Civil War rhetoric.

Authors principally interested in verbal trickery of writing are usually called formalists, which suggests how essentially serious such experiments are. Games, as everyone knows, are serious affairs, with all the trappings of rituals—fixed rules, prescribed conditions, collective participation. We have already seen how the first realistic fiction, the comic romance, grew out of formal innovations, the conventions of a seemingly exhausted genre being applied toward the invention of a new one. In a broader sense all literature is form. What makes a novel a novel, a poem a poem, a play a play, but their formal contours? Content, what the form is said to contain, as a glass contains water, is precisely what the work excludes. Smash the glass and you still have the liquid; take away the language of a book and you have blank space. "I do not paint trees," a landscape painter once remarked, "I paint pictures." The author, similarly, does not tell a life; he promotes the illusion of a life—or a divided self, or universal destruction.

In the following passage, for example, form and content are indissoluble:

Country people poor things they never saw an auto before lots of them honk the horn Candace so *She wouldn't look at me* they'll get out of the way *wouldn't look at me* your father wouldn't like it if you were to injure one of them I'll declare your father will simply have to get an auto now I'm almost sorry you brought it down Herbert I've enjoyed it so much of course there's the carriage but so often when I'd like to go out Mr Compson has the darkies doing something it would be worth my head to interrupt he insists that Roskus is at my call all the time but I know what that means I know how often people make promises just to satisfy their consciences are you going to treat my little baby girl that way Herbert but I know you wont Herbert has spoiled us all to death Quentin did I write you that he is going to take Jason into his bank when Jason finishes high school Jason will make a splendid banker he is the only one of my children with any practical sense you can thank me for that he takes after my people the others are all Compson *Jason furnished the flour. They make kites on the back porch and sold them for a nickel a piece, he and the Patterson boy. Jason was treasurer.*

This dream-like passage hardly puts us on, but is difficult to grasp. The chief obstacle is its idiosyncratic punctuation. After some emendations—removing the italicized phrases (which we'll return to), inserting some dashes, commas, and periods, and lassoing it in quotation marks—the selection looks like this:

"Country people—poor things—they never saw an auto before, lots of them. Honk the horn, Candace, so they'll get out of the way. Your father wouldn't like it if you were to injure one of them. I'll declare, your father will simply have to get an auto now. I'm almost sorry you brought it down, Herbert, I've enjoyed it so much. Of course there's the carriage; but so often when I'd like to go out, Mr. Compson has the darkies doing something it would be worth my head to interrupt. He insists that Roskus is at my call all the time, but I know what that means. I know how often people make promises just to satisfy their consciences. Are you going to treat my baby girl that way, Herbert? But I know you won't. Herbert has spoiled us all to death, Quentin. Did I write you that he is going to take Jason into his bank when Jason finishes high school? Jason will make a splendid banker. He is the only one of my children with any practical sense. You can thank me for that. He takes after my people. The others are all Compson."

So: four persons riding in a car. A woman, her son Quentin, daughter Candace, who's at the wheel, and Candace's fiancé, Herbert. We can see that the author has a reason for his manipulations. Punctuate the woman's chatter and its tone changes. It becomes a tedious, even tyrannical performance, its overspilling nervousness, unhappiness, and desperation doled out in neat clauses. It is also apparent that the italicized fragments are thoughts running through the head of the visiting son, Quentin, and must be distinguished from the monologue without staunching its flow. The entire passage, we now can see, is being recollected by Quentin; his mother's words and his own thoughts, intertwined, are unspooling in his head. The present tense makes the remembered scene more vivid; the past tense accentuates the hysterical, obsessive nature of Quentin's thoughts (these are possibly incestuous, as well: Candace "wouldn't look at me ... wouldn't look at me"). All this comes through in familiar words and perfectly captured conversational rhythms. We are in the presence of technique.

Sometimes an author can overreach in his experiments, the results, even if he's good, gratifying but costly. Here is the second half of a famous seventeenth-century poem, "Easter Wings":

> My tender age in sorrow did beginne:
> And still with sicknesses and shame
> Thou didst so punish sinne
> That I became
> Most thinne.
> With thee
> Let me combine,
> And feel this day thy victorie:
> For, if I imp my wing on thine,
> Affliction shall advance the flight in me.

The first stanza, of course, is a matching wing. As our eyes pass over these lines, we pay more attention to their look than their meaning. There are wonderful moments. "Most thinne" is a pinched little line followed by the enlarged "Let me combine," then the swelling into "victorie," and the consummation of "flight." The poem smartly executes its somersault and no less smartly exits from the mind, leaving the amused reader to scheme about designs of his own: a poem shaped like a rocket or a flower or a bottle. Its frank appeal to the eye reminds us that even in the age of literacy we retain an inner ear which we expect words to speak to. One is glad to see "Easter Wings" and thankful not to see many other poems like it.

This next and last example of experimental writing is more recent. It plays against conventional story-telling, with its fabricated "dramatic interest" and conventional "characters" whose layered "personalities" are borrowed from depth-psychology.

The brush descends the length of the loose hair with a faint noise something between the sound of a breath and a crackle. No sooner has it reached the bottom than it quickly rises again toward the head, where the whole surface of its bristles sinks in before gliding down over the black mass again. The brush is a bone-colored oval whose short handle disappears almost entirely in the hand firmly gripping it.

Half of the hair hangs down the back, the other hand pulls the other half over one shoulder. The head leans to the right, offering the hair more readily to the brush. Each time the latter lands at the top of its cycle behind the nape of the neck, the head leans farther to the right and then rises again with an effort, while the right hand, holding the brush, moves away in the opposite direction. The left hand, which loosely confines the hair between the wrist, the palm and the fingers, releases it for a second and then closes on it again, gathering the strands together with a firm, mechanical gesture, while the brush continues its course to the extreme tips of the hair. The sound, which gradually varies from one end to the other, is at this point nothing more than a dry, faint crackling, whose last sputters occur once the brush, leaving the longest hair, is already moving up the ascending part of the cycle, describing a swift curve in the air which brings it above the neck, where the hair lies flat on the back of the head and reveals the white streak of a part.

This recalls other passages we've read through a kind of opposition to them. It features a sensuous enumeration of details, like the fantasy of hell in "Voices of Prophecy," though the gulf in subject matter is so wide one can scarcely comment on it, and it has the fascination with surfaces of realism, only what realist would burden this unexceptional event with so many particulars? "She stood before the mirror, brushing her hair," would suffice, author and reader both moving on to other actions, other details. This writer rejects—even ridicules—the sense of proportion we're used to, whereby trimmings are subordinate to some larger narrative interest. With him we don't know if the brush, the hair, or the anonymous woman occupies the center of—what is this prose? a "story"? a "description"? a "report"? Its author seems a great unblinking eye, absorbing whatever falls within the radius of his undiscriminatory observation. His very detachment makes us aware of his presence, just as in documentary films the chief actor is the camera.

Making It New

Our century has seen more experimental writing than any other. Since World War I major poets, dramatists, and fiction writers have displayed uncommon interest in the forms they've chosen to work with, dismantling, discarding, reviving, reassembling. Everyone knows how poetry, which once mostly rhymed and was always metrical, has given way to "free verse," employing lines of any length and rhythms that can't be tapped out with a baton and how novels and stories, reliable vehicles of narrative, with beginnings, middles, and ends, have become prose "fictions," incident and chronology scrambled by "unreliable narrators." Heroes and villains were long ago shipped to Hollywood, which squeezed the last juices out of them (the leftover pulp is recycled in "adult" novels). Some of the best writers of our time—Jorge Luis Borges, Italo Calvino, Vladimir Nabokov to mention only a few—find imaginary cities and landscapes, the very terrain scorched by the comic romance, more expressive of human truth than the dioramas of realism. And the play, once built on the foundation of "characters" in "conflict," has become "performance art," staged events of any type. Some see in these developments simple exhaustion, the treasury of forms having been at last depleted. But such a view is shortsighted. It's like saying that the decline of the medieval church tolled the demise of spirituality, or that eroded class distinctions mean the end of public life.

No literature has been more aware of the history and traditions of literature than that written in our time. The modern author's esteem for what has gone before is what propels him in new directions, in search of new magic. As a student of the past he knows that time-burnished classics were once young and fresh and startling and that if he shirks his obligation to produce art of equal originality, he becomes a stale repeater, a crusty copier, degrading the forms he must replenish.

The writer's obligations extend beyond form. He is also, in a familiar phrase, "the antennae of the race," mandated to express the contemporary sensibility, be attuned to its changing rhythms of speech, its steadily evolving tastes, its currency of preoccupations. This was so for Homer; it must be so today. The world has changed enormously in the intervening centuries; it now seems to refurbish itself in spurts as brief as a decade. Proust, writing not so long ago—in this century—reported with amazement a recent invention which changed the texture of personal relations—the telephone. To think that instead of visiting the market one should place an order through a wire to a face one never sees, and have the meat and vegetables just arrive! Consider, too, what an astonishing development the train was. Not only were day-long journeys reduced to hours, the landscape was changed—road, house, and tree became a swirl. No wonder paintings of nature lost their static postcard appearance. We hear a modern symphony and can't understand its ugly noises, yet its inspiration may be the bleatings and booms, the daily music, of traffic snarls and planes droning overhead. Translating such multitudinous energies into language is a daunting, demanding task. The author who accepts it must strain against the limits imposed by yesterday's novels and poems and plays.

An irony of the modern age is that it has restored, through mass communications, the primacy of the performing, speaking voice. We still turn to the word for news and information, whether whispered through a wire or bounced off a satellite, but the spoken, not the written word. A hundred years ago an important part of one's regimen was reading the mail, delivered twice or even three times a day, much of it sent by nearby and intimate friends. One might meet a friend for lunch and receive that evening a note commenting on some point that had arisen in conversation. Business, as well, was conducted by letter. Literacy meant ease with the written word. Writers depended on a readership used to the "voice" that speaks to the eye. This is no longer the case. So the literary artist must find new ways of making his words vivid again.

PART TWO

BEHIND THE MASK: THE WRITER IN SOCIETY

"Every genius is defended from approach by quantities of unavailableness."

—*EMERSON*

Textual Boundaries

So far this overview of literature has included few extra-textual glances. In the case of realistic fiction a bit of history helped explain a genre devoted to the larger movements of society. In "Myself Am Hell" I cautiously speculated about the effects of the "Generalised Life" on the internal dynamics of the divided self. With visionary writing our bearings were implicit: prophecy and revelation flourish in the religious experience central to Western culture. As for the concluding thematic chapter, its topic, though amenable to comparisons with magic and games, didn't really need them. For once the reader was encouraged to think of writing purely as an art, referring only to itself. What seemed fake he could allow as fake; the totally confusing was not paraded as higher sense.

Nor has our gaze lingered on the authors of the passages at the heart of this book. This may have seemed a mistake. Not that I've sought to deny the willful intelligence behind every paragraph and line of verse; the deliberative as well as the intuitive aspects of literary invention have figured in my arguments. But I have restricted the range of inferences we were justified in drawing from a given passage. The writer's gender, age, and nationality, not to mention his marital status, social position, material circumstances—surely these would have furnished answers where we have settled for conjecture. We might have learned, for example, which of the many "I's" in this book were fabricated and which factual; we might know if they were impersonations or confessions. Yet such data have been suppressed, and for a number of reasons.

For one, our principal interest has been in coming to terms with the meaning of specific selections, a project which makes their "intention" irrelevant and distracting: words do not always serve the purposes assigned to them, even by masters. Our next concern has been with big thematic connections that traverse the artificial boundaries of "actual life." If the reader were told that a Florentine exile born in 1265 was being bracketed with an Irishman born in 1865, the capaciousness of my categories might impress him more than the intimate affinities between Dante Alighieri and William Butler Yeats. A third reason for withholding names and dates was to circumvent prejudice. There are authors trotted out so regularly in the worst sort of literary chat that one is in danger of dismissing them without benefit of acquaintanceship, just as we make a policy of avoiding people we've been told once too often we *must* meet. Finally, and most importantly, writers are not their biographical selves at the moment of inspiration. They become instead what they write. Personality doesn't disappear into the text; it is, rather, the fiber which gives each voice its peculiar and familiar consistency (or *texture*). No work can engage us unless we respond to the personality of its author, but personality itself is never enough. An author's life and loves, his "civilian" career, can be disappointingly commonplace. Only when his experience passes through the alembic of invention, emerging as formalized language, does it lay any lasting claim on our interest.

There is one non-textual question which this handbook can rightfully address, the place of the writer in the larger scheme of things. The plain fact that it is a question, posed alike by writer and reader and, especially, non-reader, justifies a brief examination. The writer, with each succeeding generation, holds a more elusive position in our culture. We expect him to entertain and enlighten us, we lavish celebrity and money on him, but grant him no authority. Nowhere is this ambivalence more apparent than in our response to the major works of our own time. The disgust with which many of us greet difficult or "obscure" novels and plays (most poetry gets no greeting at all), our unrelieved exasperation and indignation, suggests that we expect a great deal from our writers, as if the ancient office of elucidating the mystery of existence, of shaping phenomena in the crucible of metaphor, persists in our thoughts as something between a hope and a regret. Is a new book of truths being written today, we wonder in moments of enthusiasm for the age, a new *Iliad* or Bible? Then the haze is burned away by despair and we produce remarks like, "Everything's already been said by Shakespeare. Why bother to read anything new?" What this really means is that something hasn't been said, and the likelihood that it will be diminishes daily.

I have spoken of literature's power to transform our lives. I didn't mention the word most often invoked by our personal hopes: happiness. We expect books to crystallize for us the conditions of happiness, to establish in their rival world a model which we can borrow and apply to our own circumstances. The very exclusiveness of literary art, its reduction of humanity into characters, its planning of bumpy lives into smooth stories, its cosmic revelations contained within the distance between two words, is what we ache to learn from. Many of us turn to books of the past, finding in them the coherence, the straightforward approach to serious matters, that the appointed antennae of our own epoch appear to scorn. Others prefer the superficial amusements of bestsellers. And yet the more one reads, the less certain the certitudes become. The comfortable old classics seem less simple than one remembered; for as we grow complicated we complicate all we touch. And the pleasing quick surfaces of popular current fiction seem neither pleasing nor satisfying. Suddenly a single criterion looms above every other in our estimation of a book. What does it give me after the first reading? Does it change as I change? Do its revelations still obtain? The only happiness a book can provide, we begin to suspect, is the happiness of reading it. This happiness is not identical with stimulation (as love is not identical to lust), nor with contentedness (which is too placid, like a snoozing cat); the happiness we find reading comes from pleasurable engagement of imagined worlds.

The consequences of literature can be great; as the writer's invention gains reality, "actual life" loses it: facts breed metaphors; analysis crumbles before intuition; waking life seems the shadow of a dream. Reading then becomes a crucial and elemental activity, a remaking of the world. This remaking binds literature to "actual life" even as it brings them into collision. For the author's bending of content into form echoes the basic experiment of society itself, with its collective application of form (the poet's "things") to our own rough beings. The results attained by these parallel efforts are almost always at odds, but necessarily so, as illusion and reality are necessarily opposed: neither has meaning without the other. We proceed now to a rapid glimpse of the reciprocal effect of the writer and his culture. How has he shaped it and how has it shaped him?

Privileged Voices

In ancient days authors were regarded as crafts-men, working with language as other artificers worked with silver or gold. The greatest poets were revered, and the beauty of their verse was a source of national pride and universal truth, but the inventors them-selves remained elusive figures embedded in their work and no one gave much thought to what they did or were when not composing. As we've already seen, Homer's name, despite its lofty cultural position, is affixed to a mass of conjecture. What we haven't known hasn't mattered. In antiquity the author, as a rule, wasn't interesting, but his representation of the world outside himself was. He received—what celebrity so often denies—serious attention. In Athens's "golden age," beginning in the fifth century B.C., writers were consulted in times of crisis—war or famine—and their predictive power judged supernal. The poet's eccen-tricity (literally, his "off-centeredness") connoted secret knowledge unavailable to the experts who actually ran things. Citizens flocked to plays by Aristophanes and

128

Euripides, not only for amusement, but for opinions and counsel. These were not always dispensed gently; leaders and policy came in for sharp rebuke or ridicule. The poet was neither punished for his point of view nor personally credited with superior gifts of reason. The wisdom that infused his work was something he couldn't claim responsibility for. If the gods spoke through his words it was because he had been nominated to convey divine insight. This notion, like so many things Greek, was adopted by the Romans, with some pragmatic alterations. They hit upon the practice of subsidizing poets to endorse official policy. They needn't be blatant about it—no odes to the status quo were required, only a gallant bow to the emperor. Virgil's *Aeneid* pays respects to Augustus without compromising its high standards; and Horace, though rewarded in his thirties with a farm, didn't permit his indebtedness (to the patron Maecenas) to palliate his sorrowful lyrics or take the bite out of his satires.

Well into the Middle Ages poets and kings continued to serve one another, with the church as intermediary. In those days of minimal literacy, fluent readers and writers were scarce outside monastic orders. The ruler who needed assistance with his "paperwork"—edicts, reforms, legal judgments, etc.—turned to the church, which was quite willing to have its clerics installed inside the palace walls, privy to affairs of state and often involved in them. The theologian and versifier Alcuin of York headed Charlemagne's palace school, instructing the emperor, his family, and courtiers and had a hand in composing royal documents. In return he received revenues from monasteries which fell within his employer's demesne, and retired to a comfortable abbey.

The king couldn't house or employ every talented writer. Patronage, whereby poets, as well as painters and musicians, received stipends from lower nobility, evolved as a basic feature of medieval society, and lasted for centuries. A fascinating court career was that of the fifteenth-century poet Christine de Pizan, who wrote prolifically about love, religion, morality, history, politics, and women. Her success was without precedent, since she lived in a time of rigid social roles. Not only was a woman's place in the home; even there her behavior followed a prescribed pattern. Solemn treatises were regularly published informing young brides of their marital obligations: they should be sure to cook their husbands' preferred dishes; greet them in crisp and pretty frocks; speak to them soothingly and lovingly, no matter what indecencies they committed; and ask few questions. Prevailing wisdom held it dangerous for women to be taught to read.

Given this state of affairs, Christine's career is astonishing; luck—good and bad—played a considerable part in it. The good luck was that her father, a professor and astrologer at the University of Bologna, won the attention and favor of King Charles V of France, and was invited to join the royal court in Paris. There the Pizan family held a choice position, Christine's father perusing the stars while Christine read in the palace library. Her father must have been a liberal man, because he encouraged her studies. The king, too, evidently approved of this literary young woman. In 1379, at age sixteen, Christine married Charles's secretary and notary. Life looked promising. But not for long. A year after her marriage the king died, and heirs wrangled over the throne. In the confusion the Pizan family lost its position, and her father, plunged into arrears, suffered a long and fatal illness. Christine's young husband soon followed him to the grave, leaving his widow with three children and no prospects. In desperation she initiated a suit to reclaim her family's lost income and property, and, as it got tangled in red tape, retreated into the solace of lucubration, reading widely and deeply in poetry, history, and science. In the hope of winning a reputation and the support of a patron, Christine embarked on original projects. Luck again: she had talent. Her works were noticed and a number of noble sponsors, including the royal family (an heir having at last emerged), expressed interest. Christine's head did not swell: more than once she modestly suggested that her celebrity owed more to novelty than to skill. So rare was a woman writer then that suspicious (and, assuredly, envious) rivals sought to expose her as an imposter, their "evidence" based solely on the premise that no woman could write so well.

No doubt this treatment contributed to Christine's feminism. She wrote a history of great women called *The Book of the City of Ladies*, an account of Joan of Arc, and much verse and prose decrying the plight of widows. She was most celebrated for her participation in a famous literary debate about the French medieval classic, Jean de Meun's *The Romance of the Rose*, accused by Christine of defaming women. She also wrote moral and religious treatises for the general public, and a biography of Charles V. Vowing fidelity to the memory of her husband, Christine never remarried. She spent her last days in a convent, where she died at seventy. Though her writings were reissued and translated throughout the next century, her reputation subsequently faltered. The modern age, however, has caught up to this remarkable woman: as I write, a reissue of *The Book of the City of Ladies* is finding its way into bookstores.

The Birth of the Vernacular

By the fourteenth century, when Christine began her career, Europe was entering the Renaissance, an epoch, as we saw in "Things as They Are," of social and cultural revolution. An early sign that medieval horizons were widening was the growth of literature composed not in Latin but in the spoken, or "vulgar," tongues of Europe. Christine, for instance, wrote in

French. Two centuries before she would not have done so, especially when addressing moral and religious matters. The way for her and other serious vernacular writers was paved by troubadours, who performed—reciting, singing, acting—in their native tongues. Despite its popularity, vulgar literature was not officially esteemed until the Crusades, when the church discovered that rousing ballads, though unfit for the canon of divine writing, helped swell the recruitment ranks.

Not long after troubadours gained in influence, learned writers began to ponder the possibilities offered by the vernacular. It was not easy confining oneself to Latin, a language seldom spoken outside the church, and even then only in—who could deny it?—debased form. The great classics of Roman antiquity—Virgil, Horace, and Ovid—though pagans, were, nonetheless, far superior to any poets of the early Middle Ages. And was this not an embarrassment to Christianity, a sublime religion without a sublime poetry?

A hundred years before Christine's birth the city of Florence, destined to become the jewel of the Renaissance, produced a vernacular poet who not only rivaled but surpassed the known masters of antiquity. Dante Alighieri did not write his masterpiece in his native city, although he did compose his first major work there, *La Vita nuova (The New Life)*, in his twenties. This work of poetry and prose was itself an event in Western literature, for in it Dante celebrated his love for a flesh-and-blood woman, Beatrice, in daring images linking the spiritual and the physical (he actually equated her with Christ), and signaled the advent of a new Christian literature, praising God and the material world with equal fervor. This achievement behind him, he was for a time deflected from his vocation by his passionate involvement in political and church struggles which led to his banishment from Florence in 1302. Thereafter he roamed Italy, serving one court after another, in various intellectual and advisory capacities, dreaming all the while of a triumphant return to the city he pined for. *La Commedia* (posterity added *Divina* two centuries later) was written over fourteen years. It is not only the first sublime post-classical work; it remains the most influential and beautiful poem ever written. We saw one passage from it, the chilling account of the serpent and the three thieves. Dante succeeded prodigiously in establishing Italian as a language equal to its progenitor, Latin, but he didn't work alone. Other poets, chiefly his contemporary and friend Guido Cavalcanti, helped invent a "sweet new style" exploring the music of the spoken tongue.

Doubts about the vernacular lingered long after the Middle Ages. As late as the seventeenth century, John Milton, whose adolescent lyrics were written in Greek and Latin, feared that by composing *Paradise Lost* in English he might sacrifice a world reputation. Using the vernacular meant, in a demonstrable way, rejecting the language of God, a strange move for a poet inspired to "justify the ways of God to men." It further confined one's readership to one's own countrymen at a time when Europe was still proudly unified in its Latin heritage. Even in the latter decades of the eighteenth century, when Samuel Johnson visited France, he thought it proper to converse not in French, which he knew fluently, but in Latin.

The Printing Press and the Mass Market

A really wide readership did not exist before the Renaissance. Court poets and troubadours had the attention of influential people, but only a few at a time, and reputations traveled slowly. Manuscripts were copied and circulated—some, like the anonymous *Song of Roland* (originally an oral poem, the most renowned of the French *chansons de geste*, or "songs of heroic deeds"), Chrétien de Troyes's romances, *The Divine Comedy*, Boccaccio's *Decameron*, and the poems of Chaucer, finding big audiences. But it was the printing press, Western civilization's first mass-production machine, invented by Johannes Gensfleisch (who called himself Gutenberg) that disseminated books to the population at large. Not that literature was instantly transformed. The sudden availability of books meant an increase in literacy alarming to the aristocracy, whose power rested in part on an ignorant serfdom, and to the priesthood, whose status as interpreters of the divine word owed much to their exclusive ability to read sacred texts. In addition, scribes and manuscript illuminators, fearful of competition from this newfangled apparatus, made a clever case for its being heretical in its duplication of images, and sponsored laws that made setting a book in type a transgression of ecclesiastical authority.

To the rescue came that unfastidious and brazen crew, the middle class, learning to read and greedy for affordable books (imagine what a personally scribed tome must have cost). In towns and cities throughout the continent, the bourgeoisie subsidized presses. Books were hardly spewing forth: in the fifteenth century editions ran to about two hundred copies. Still, this invention added new meaning to the laws of supply and demand: as quickly as the first small printing sold out, another was under way. The first bestseller, Thomas à Kempis's *De imitatione Christi (The Imitation of Christ)* had gone into ninety-nine printings by the year 1500. Gradually, printed books found acceptance, and were available in numbers that altered the course of literature.

The first English printer was William Caxton, a successful businessman (or, as the guild he belonged to put it, "Merchant Adventurer") whose work took him to the Continent. He set up a publishing company in Cologne, translating popular French works, but soon discovered the inefficiencies of peddling them from across the Channel and moved his operation to

London, where from 1476 to 1492, the year of his death, he published at a furious pace, churning out updated classics, religious tracts, and romances. His chief innovation was to preface each volume with a spurious dedication singing its praises, gulling readers into thinking it the favorite of Lord So-and-so and thus the height of literary fashion. Today such packaged encomiums flourish as blurbs.

Another development of this time was the rage for heroic romances, those improbable tales involving a hermit, a shipwreck, and a wood, or knights, castles, and maidens. These were based on medieval chronicles, but, since the dream of feudal glory had ended with the bloody disasters of the Crusades, the genre seemed, to critical readers, both nostalgic and contrived. As we've seen, refurbishing the conventions of the heroic romance led to the modern novel. I identified this development with England and the eighteenth century. In fact, long before Dr. Johnson was moved to write his essay, the comic romance was anticipated by a Spaniard.

Miguel de Cervantes Saavedra's life spanned the same decades as Shakespeare's, though far more tumultuously. He was chamberlain, or treasurer, to a cardinal, served in the navy, and twice was imprisoned—first by Turks, who captured him in battle and locked him up in Algiers for five years; the second occasion was less heroic. As commissary to the Spanish Navy he was caught with his hand in the till. During this latter stint he began a parody of popular fiction, *Don Quixote*. This astonishing book was an instantaneous hit, as masterpieces often are, and made its author famous. Unfortunately copyright laws had scarcely evolved, and pirated copies kept the author from turning a profit. In fact, he found himself writing at a desperate rate to keep ahead of fraudulent "sequels."

Don Quixote recounts the misadventures of a mad hidalgo so consumed with passion for heroic romances and enthralled by the dream of gallant knighthood that he takes to the road in the hope of performing splendid deeds of his own, everywhere he goes meddling in events he has hopelessly misapprehended. He is literature's preeminent sucker for appearances, so often and easily duped that in his confusion he succeeds in remaking the world around him. For midway through his novel the author makes a discovery about the don: his preposterous misreadings, stoked by his illusions, alter the aspect of things. This discovery, we have seen, lies behind all great fiction, right up through Proust. What seems to be, even or especially to the wildest eyes, actually is, because in our conviction that a windmill is a giant, or a tainted inheritance a grand dispensation, we grant them, and ourselves, new identities.

Cervantes was a well-educated man, who had mastered numerous forms and styles. But, like his great contemporary Shakespeare, he did not feel enslaved to tradition. He viewed it no less shrewdly than he viewed the audience whose tastes and illusions he ridiculed, sometimes cruelly, in his novel. His insouciance freed Cervantes to outdo even Dante in one respect:

he invented single-handed a literary form, the realistic novel. Much time elapsed before other writers caught up with him. Not until the eighteenth century would worthy English apprentices, like Henry Fielding (an avowed disciple of Cervantes) and Laurence Sterne, write their own comedies of romance.

The Classical Tradition Sustained

The advent of the novel did not abruptly terminate the court tradition. In France, bastion of feudalism, the classical mode continued well into the seventeenth century, culminating in the cultural apogee of Louis XIV's Versailles. Writers like Madame de Sévigné and the Duc de Saint-Simon and La Rochefoucauld forged a classic modern prose, and two playwrights, one a tragedian, the other a comedian, made the stage nearly as vibrant as Shakespeare had done across the Channel. Jean Racine's dramas, *Phèdre* and *Andromaque* among others, adhered with impressive fidelity to Aristotelian principles of formal unity and thematic grandeur. His stories fuse ancient myths with modern moral dilemmas, and his heroes are demi-gods with a psychological dimension rooted in realism. Just as Racine's protagonists struggle against their own baseness to reach nobility, the plays themselves strain against their formal rigidities; this dynamism can make Racine seem stilted, though he is often called the last true tragedian in Western literature. The comedies of Molière—*Tartuffe, Don Juan, The Misanthrope*—are scintillating farces of manners and ideas. One senses in Molière's extravagant villains the emergence of new men—ambitious courtiers, manipulating narcissists, hypocritical moralists—precise foreshadowings, in a different social context, of types lampooned a century later in the English novel.

In the following century, as we saw in "Things as They Are," a new view of society came into being. A landed economy controlled by wealthy renters, who acquired their property through strict laws of inheritance, gave way to the mercantile capitalism of investors, manufacturers, and traders. Money rivaled acreage as the measure of fortunes; assets became fluid. A society patterned after the fluctuations of francs or pounds begins itself to fluctuate, and writers shrewdly took note. Novelists, in tales of social adventure or closely observed studies of manners, commented on the intricacies of a protean society and the difficulty of finding in it stable virtues.

Poets, beholden to a classical heritage, were even more ambivalent. They were glad to be liberated from the old system of patronage, and willing to offer their wares on the marketplace. (Until our own century poetry sold surprisingly well; even in the middle years of the last century its sales matched those of fiction.) But the serious poet had come to rely on a cultivated audience, with superior taste and knowledge of literature, and this readership was dwindling. Catering to a badly educated public compromised the artist no less than flattering noble patrons. In addition, poets faced the consequences of secular thought. As early as the fifteenth century the Polish astronomer Copernicus had challenged biblical assumptions with his careful mappings of planetary movements. His evidence that the sun, and not the earth, was the fixed center of the heavens was so revolutionary that he did not issue his findings until he lay on his deathbed, leaving subsequent generations to grapple with them. New revelations provided by the telescope confirmed and refined the Copernican theory and led to further trespasses against received ideas. Soon theology, once the highest "science," was replaced by astronomy, and, later, physics, biology, and chemistry. If the new economy had begun to weaken the old hierarchical structure, fresh knowledge finished it off.

The Renaissance was modulated into bourgeois individualism by the Enlightenment. Its principal figures—Bacon, Descartes, Spinoza, Voltaire, Rousseau, Locke, Newton, Hume—arrived at a rational, rather than a spiritual, conception of the universe, with Man displacing God at its center. The poet, who from antiquity had been esteemed for his mysterious intuition of the divine, lost his privileged status to the man who made things work, from governments to machines. Thus America, a grand Enlightenment

141

project, has always honored its engineers—Edison and Bell—before its pioneers of the imagination.

How could poets reconcile these new developments with their spiritual leanings? The greatest poet after Shakespeare, Milton, offered little guidance. His astonishing achievement—an epic that almost ranked with Dante's and Homer's—frightened away potential successors and drove home a painful point: to be a major voice in this age one had to be a genius. Milton himself certainly had been. Milton, who as a Cambridge undergraduate composed some of the most precocious poems in the language; who, upon graduation, imprisoned himself in his father's library, mastering not only English but also Hebrew, Greek, Latin, and Italian literature; who met and conversed with Galileo (saluted, in *Paradise Lost*, as "the Tuscan artist"); who, in his frenzy of pamphleteering in support of Oliver Cromwell, read and wrote himself blind, so that when he came to invent his amazing poem he had to recite it, like Homer himself, to his amanuensis. No poet, steeped in the majestic blank verse of *Paradise Lost*, could hope to rival or surpass it; and yet to aspire to anything less was to forfeit one's claim to ultimate seriousness. After 1674, the year of his death, Milton cast an intimidating shadow over English poetry.

As one might expect, the next major poets differed sharply from Milton, veering toward verse that in many ways resembled prose. John Dryden and Alexander Pope employed rhymed couplets that accommodated humor, wit, and technical display. Their work was formally fastidious and satirical in content, playing a lofty classicism against the base realities of their day, much as the novel was to do later. But for all its skill and resourcefulness the "mock-heroic" style sacrificed the enrapturing magic of visionary poetry. Oddly enough, it was Milton himself who provided an escape from Fear of Milton. Eighteenth-century poets like William Collins and Thomas Gray discovered in his early poems, particularly "Lycidas," "L'Allegro," and "Il Penseroso," a route back to visionary writing via the ode and the elegy and signaled a new subject for the poet: himself. Poets began to address in verse the difficulties of writing when they felt no longer aided by tradition but stymied by it, needful of strategies for recovering mystery in the face of scientific fact, uncertain about the place of poetry in an increasingly secular world.

The Writer as Person

In the eighteenth century the marketplace made literary success a matter of quick popularity, of the book that caught the public fancy, running into multiple printings, stirring controversy. I mentioned earlier how readers of realistic novels were passionately attached to their fictional blood kin, their Pamelas and Clarissas and Tom Joneses. Naturally, authors too were engulfed in this tide of interest. Who were these men who knew so much about what was whispered behind closed doors, who parodied so ingeniously coffee-house chatter?

The first great literary biographer in English was someone now familiar to the reader, Samuel Johnson. The Doctor, whose prodigious erudition, moral intelligence, and handsome prose bestrode the middle decades of the eighteenth century, had for many years buttered his bread with hackwork. There was nothing hypocritical in this. For one thing, he hadn't much choice, living as he did in constant poverty. Poverty had forced him to leave Oxford, where he was a brilliant student with a preternatural memory for verse; poverty had led him to found a private school when in his twenties; poverty was the result when this effort failed. Secondly, Johnson's hackwork was very good, good enough to justify his famous remark that anyone who writes for anything but money is a fool. Nonetheless, he was pleased and relieved when a royal pension conferred on him an annuity of 300 pounds, freeing him from the necessity of earning a living by his pen.

Johnson is an interesting case of the new kind of writer—learned and gifted, yet dependent on the public for his livelihood. Luckily, the public then craved useful books. What made his name was his *Dictionary of the English Language* (published in 1755; its definition of "pension": "money given to a State hireling for treason to his country"), a venture he undertook without collaborators, paid consultants, or research assistants. At the same time he wrote poems, reviews, and essays like "The Comedy of Romance." Another early project was his biography of a now almost forgotten poet, his friend Richard Savage, a rakehell

> whose writings entitle him to an eminent rank in the classes of learning, and whose misfortunes claim a degree of compassion not always due to the unhappy, as they were often the consequences of the crimes of others rather than his own.

Johnson's supreme biographical achievement was his last major work, *The Lives of the Poets*, commissioned by booksellers when he was in his seventies as introductions to more than fifty recent poets, from Milton to Gray, each consisting of a biography and critical assessment. The biography for which Dr. Johnson is best known, however, is the classic telling of his own life by James Boswell. *The Life of Samuel Johnson, LL.D.*, one of the monuments of our language, has affinities with another emergent literary form we've had prior cause to consider, the realistic novel. Through scrupulous attention to detail, an abundance of dining-room and drawing-room and "on-the-road" adventures, and above all a willingness to let his subject discourse freely on a broad spectrum of topics, from the classics to cats, Boswell made high drama and splendid comedy of Johnson's life, and captured as well the flavor of an era. So successful was Boswell that for many years, well into our century, Johnson was better remembered as protagonist than as author.

Toward the end of the eighteenth century, public fascination with the lives of writers and the writer's own growing interest in himself merged into an exalted idea of the writer as hero. The poets chiefly responsible for this development were the Romantics, the first and most unusual of whom was William Blake. Born in 1757, the son of a London hosier, Blake received no formal education, although he studied drawing as a child and was apprenticed to an engraver. With this skill, plus his talents as an illustrator, Blake earned the small income that enabled him to work on his own poetry, printed by himself. His books are exquisite, not just for their great poetry, but for their typesetting and lovely illuminations. Other poets came to him with their work, and the editions he produced were cherished by the few who saw them. He died penniless, attended by his wife, who was remarkable in her own right. She had been illiterate when they married; under her husband's tutelage she learned to write in his vigorous style, assisted on his often wonderful (though typically idiosyncratic and under-appreciated) paintings, and conducted his correspondence.

We have already seen a morsel of Blake's startling verse, with its fervid talk of decay and regeneration and biblical tone. Blake was saturated in the Bible, whose myth of a fall and resurrection he retold in secular terms. Long before anthropology emerged to codify myths, establishing them as a foundation of culture, Blake held that the imaginative faculty is part of our equipment for comprehending phenomena. The minimal prestige modern society affords the imagination isn't, Blake knew, the result of progress or "rational thought," but a proof of intellectual timidity; the self that reads the world, and not its own theories superimposed over it, always reveres intuition and perception. Blake thought the project of the new visionary must no longer be transmitting God's word, but tapping into human energies suppressed by social and intellectual machinery. It's not surprising that he was an early believer in social revolution (and a friend of Tom Paine), heartened by the events of 1776 and 1789, nor that he lapsed into disillusionment when he saw how unspiritual those uprisings proved to be.

The French Revolution was a crucial occurrence in the lives and minds of Romantics, for whom it heralded the opportunity for humankind to reshape the world in an image of freedom, bringing utopian visions to fruition. Earlier generations had felt the impossibility of retaining faith in social harmony as an inherited social structure crumbled under the pressures of secularism, but for intellectuals of the revolutionary generation the toppling of the old system seemed rich in promise. Perhaps a renewed state would allow persons to control their own destinies, bound not by hierarchy but by a shared belief in "liberty, equality, fraternity," and the infinite capacities of Man. Sadly the initial glory of revolution turned to conflagration from which rose the imperial specter of Napoleon, dashing many hopes. In England there was the further disappointment of the government's conservative reaction to events overseas. The hope of a brave new world seemed faint. There was still the prospect for change held out by America, but who were those "rebels" really but a merchant cabal grousing about taxes? As for its great men—Washington, Jefferson, Franklin—they were just bourgeois anti-monarchists, well-heeled Calvinists with some ideas borrowed from Locke.

So much for conventional politics. There was still the spirit. Even the sour turn of events did not undermine a powerful surge of hope for the future. The *future*: the very word rang with new meaning; the coming age would no longer be charted by an omniscient, invisible Engineer but hammered out by visionaries. The literature of the nineteenth century reflects an era of social reform, of cooperative movements, of public schools, "perfectability." In literature this meant a restoration of the gift of prophecy and revelation, a renovated belief in the spirit derived no longer from the biblical covenant (though, as Blake showed, its myths and language could thrive) but from the drama imposed by man's attempt to wreak his will on, or against, nature.

The two greatest Romantics were Johann Wolfgang von Goethe and William Wordsworth, a pair of names that go together strangely. Goethe towers over the second half of the eighteenth century and the first quarter of the nineteenth. He wrote novels, plays, poems, opera librettos, travel books, scientific studies. Fame found him early with the publication of his epistolary novel, *The Sorrows of Young Werther*, the story of an inwardly divided young man driven to abasement and suicide. There had never been a novel like *Werther* and it took Europe by storm. Young men modeled themselves on its passionate protagonist whose soul is bared to beauty until it is swamped by pain. Here was an unprecedented conception of man, living in exquisite anguish, silhouetted against the sky. Goethe's masterpiece is *Faust*, a dramatic poem based on the traditional story of a learned doctor who barters his soul to the devil in exchange for that magical Romantic triad: youth, knowledge, and power. Man is not in these works simply the highest creature in a long "chain of being," the beast nearest God. He himself harbors the divine and its opposite; he is thinker and animal, mind and body. This was an idea that had been steadily spreading through Europe. It was born in the seventeenth century; we glimpsed it in our brief mention of French classical drama, with its heroes struggling to surmount their own baseness as they seek noble destinies. But the Romantics lifted this idea to new limits.

Youth, knowledge, and power also figure in the poetry of Wordsworth, but in a much different way. Unlike Goethe, Wordsworth labored in obscurity for most of his career, though embraced early by a coterie of discerning readers and lauded by other writers as England's most potent and original voice since Milton.

His enormous influence on two successive generations of poets—that of Shelley and Keats, and that of Browning and Tennyson and Matthew Arnold—carried his renown to a larger audience and in 1843, at age seventy-three, the muse having long since deserted him, Wordsworth was named Poet Laureate. But it was in the decade from 1798 to 1808, in lyrics like "Intimations of Immortality," "Tintern Abbey," and "Resolution and Independence," and in his fourteen-book autobiographical epic *The Prelude*, that Wordsworth made poetry once again a medium of spiritual power. No poet did more to establish nature as both the background for and the projection of poetic consciousness; and no poet since, except possibly Yeats, has equaled Wordsworth's philosophical freshness. In contrast to his coeval Blake, Wordsworth proposed no schematic representation of Man and his Fall and Regeneration. His gifts were aimed at what might be called a gentling of the visionary impulse. A great psychologist; he understood that the apocalyptic experience is a frightening challenge to our psychic need for continuity and internal order. Often in his poems crises emerge from the sudden apprehension of the terror held out by nature. Just when Wordsworth's poetic persona verges on a perception that may unhinge him, he finds some lowly object or being—a stone or an aged tramp, something equally imbued with solid irrefutable presence—that binds his insight to more common intuitions and feelings. Wordsworth's characteristic tone has not the thunder of Isaiah, quoted in "Voices of Prophecy," but the quiet stillness of the visionary aftermath, as in the Book of Kings, though as latter-day visions Wordsworth's crises all occur within the mind.

Romanticism and Realism

Where does the realistic novel fit into the nineteenth century's rediscovery of the visionary faculty? How does a form dedicated to detailing the mechanics of the social life, with its mappings of material progress, chime with the utopian tilt of poetry? We must return to the Romantic triad: youth, knowledge, and power. That is where the novelist and the poet converge.

The poet's absorption in the spiritual quest was best expressed in attempts to come to terms with nature (a concrete example of this: the fragment of verse cited in "Voices of Prophecy," which imaged a landscape as a sick human corpse, uniting earth and flesh in a vision of animality). The novelist conducted his search for revelation within limits offered by the social world. *Great Expectations*, for instance, with its misreading adventurer ennobled by the intensity of his illusions, explores the relation of belief to knowledge, and tests the power of a "character" to live out his dreams of the ideal life. As for youth: is Pip really innocent, or is he overenamored of the possibilities held out by wealth? And at what point does he cease to be young and innocent? When he severs old ties? When he learns the "truth"?

The novel, to a great extent, brought together the realistic and the romantic, the visionary faculty and the art of copying. A master of this mingling of viewpoints was Honoré de Balzac, whose vast and panoramic series, *The Human Comedy*, depicts through unrivaled attention to minute detail the hectic energy of bourgeois France, particularly Paris and its ambitious dreamers and plotters. His amazing eye for the telling emblem—of clothing, furniture, human feature—makes his scenes bristling miniatures of a teeming society and his representation of society as an organic process analogous to nature owed much to visionary literature.

A unique blending of realism and Romanticism, or more accurately of the novel and poetry, was accomplished by Emily Brontë. She lived only thirty years, and wrote just one classic, *Wuthering Heights*, but in it she gave a heavy Victorian plot wonderful intensity. Its lovers consumed by a kind of holy and doomed passion, its brooding landscape, its febrile prose unite visionary power with psychological depth. Yet the unraveling of the yarn and the cast of supporting characters are in keeping with the inclusiveness of the "standard" Victorian novel.

Three novelists took the form to unprecedented heights. Gustave Flaubert's *Madame Bovary* (1853–57), the story of a doomed young adulteress, captured the banality of bourgeois culture in exquisitely honed details (a ridiculous hat, a cab ride, dung outside a farmhouse). Count Leo Tolstoy was a magisterial intelligence who roamed with ease over a vast range of experience in *War and Peace* (1865–69), a modern epic in which world history is balanced against the subtle stresses of family life, and in *Anna Karenina* (1875–77), whose passionate heroine is pitted against the cruel supermachinery of conventional values. Engagement in the social fray exacts its heaviest toll on our inner beings, as we saw in "Myself Am Hell." The exultant voice in that chapter belonged to Tolstoy's contemporary Fyodor Dostoevsky the greatest psychologist in all of literature. His comprehension of dark regions of the psyche in novels like *Crime and Punishment*, *The Possessed*, and *The Brothers Karamazov*, put the capstone on the Romantic project of absorbing the universe into the mind. Dostoevsky's characters, gripped by shame and desire, needful of others yet driven to abasement, possessed by evil though yearning for redemption, express the unappeasable duality of humankind. The divided self—the Enlightenment obsession which produced *Paradise Lost*, the visions of Blake, and the ruminations of Goethe and Wordsworth—is portrayed in Dostoevsky's fiction with a complexity matched only later by the grand mythology of Freud.

Unacknowledged Legislators

The most important legacy of Romanticism was that it gave novelists and poets alike an exhilarating sense of themselves as authorities, as the great voices of their time. Writers boasted of their status as seeers and seers, chroniclers and prophets, just as civilization at large had once perceived them. In a famous phrase the poet Shelley declared that writers, with a special access to language and thus to thought, were "the unacknowledged legislators" of the world. And his compatriot and contemporary Keats, writing to his brother and sister-in-law, who had emigrated to the New World, refers to a mutual friend who

> pleases himself with the idea that America will be the country to take up the human intellect where england leaves off—I differ there with him greatly—A country like the united states whose greatest Men are Franklins and Washingtons will never do that—They are great Men doubtless but how are they to be compared to Milton...?

What's interesting is not Keats's opinion of America but his idea of who properly qualifies to "take up the human intellect," who, as he notes later in this sinuous sentence, "reach[es] the sublime." The sublime: spiritual power. The hopes of the nineteenth century resuscitated a quality moribund just a hundred years before. And it is true that when we total up the great statesmen of the last century perhaps only one—Lincoln—does not pale alongside the litany of artists and intellectual legislators—Goethe and Tolstoy and Ibsen and Beethoven and Wagner and Darwin and Whitman and Hegel and Marx. The difference is not one of tangible influence, but of "the human intellect." It is artists and thinkers, rather than doers, who seem to represent, to stand for, their time, or rather against it: the unacknowledged legislator seldom is enrolled in the party of power.

And yet the Romantics' celebration of themselves as exemplary beings had an ironic result. At the very moment authors were feeling their strength, they were being absorbed into the "Generalised Life."

No writer in history lived more in the public eye, and closer to the center of political tempests, than Lord Byron. Like Goethe, Byron achieved fame in his early twenties, when he published the first two cantos of *Childe Harold's Pilgrimage*, a rambling autobiographical poem similar in some respects to a comic romance. Other books followed, equally popular. In 1814 a volume of his poetry, *The Corsair*, sold ten thousand copies on the day of publication, a staggering figure even by today's standards. Byron's success had no precedent. And it was international; if anything, he was more admired on the Continent than at home, where scandal and gossip always nipped at his heels. He had many love affairs, not always conventional. Rumors of incest and his wife's insistence on a separation, in addition to his disgust with British conservatism, persuaded him to forsake his homeland in 1816, at the age of twenty-eight. There were not many years left to him: he fell fatally ill and died in 1824, assisting Greek insurgents in their struggle for independence from Turkey. He left behind some of the most wonderful letters in English, and an unfinished masterpiece, *Don Juan*, which combines epic, confession, and social satire. Byron was less interested in being a major poet than in being a hero, someone whom others would not only read but pattern their lives after. He came closer to realizing this aim than any author has since.

By the middle of the last century the publicizing trend had set in. Dickens made a profitable tour of the United States in 1867. Twenty years later Matthew Arnold, important as a poet but as a critic England's chief arbiter of taste and "high seriousness," made his American tour. On the East Coast, in the Midwest, and in the South he lectured to hushed halls packed with literati, local dignitaries, common laborers. Everyone wanted to hear the distinguished emissary of culture and what he thought of an upstart nation and its literature. Why wasn't his estimation of Emerson higher? What did he think of Mark Twain? The most memorable American tour was probably Oscar

Wilde's, in 1882. Not yet a major writer, he was chiefly known as the flamboyant personality satirized by Gilbert and Sullivan in their comic opera, *Patience*, recommendation enough for impresarios to send him on a round of lectures in places like Kansas City and Leadville, the Colorado mining town, where

> the amazement of the miners when they saw that art and appetite could go hand in hand knew no bounds; when I lit a long cigar they cheered till the silver fell in dust from the roof on our plates; and when I quaffed a cocktail without flinching, they unanimously pronounced me in their grand simple way "a bully boy with no glass eye"—artless and spontaneous praise which touched me more than the pompous panegyrics of literary critics ever did or could.

Of course celebrity was not the lot of every writer; only a handful, as in our own time, ever became household names. And even those who were famous didn't necessarily reap financial rewards. Arnold, despite his heavily promoted tour, banked just enough income to ease the burden of his old age after years of toil as a school inspector, sleeping and eating in dismal inns in strange towns, with little free time to write. And there were writers who simply preferred anonymity, shunning the public eye, working in quiet solitude—particularly in the latter half of the century, when the Romantic dream faded and the shroud of Victorian stolidity had settled over Europe and America.

It is strange to think that our country, with its addiction to publicity and celebrity, should have produced perhaps the most extraordinary unacknowledged legislator of the nineteenth century. But Emily Dickinson chose to live as a recluse, writing beautiful and elusive lyrics hidden from the public until after she died. She was born in 1830 in Amherst, Massachusetts, and passed nearly all her life there. She received her education nearby, then returned to her parents' house, seldom venturing beyond its walls. There is much dispute about why she opted for such extreme reclusiveness: an unhappy love affair? renunciation of the world of experience? And why, shortly before withdrawing, did she begin to dress always and only in white? So gifted a writer defeats curiosity; she is puzzling to us but not to herself.

Her poems are unlike any others in English. It's as if she invented writing, without having glanced at masters or models. Not that her short lyrics seem untutored or clumsy. They are just the opposite: marvelously rhythmical, with subtle off-rhymes and an almost algebraic perfection of form, the musings of a shrewd mind delighted by complexities and paradox yet pitched to a high intensity. Most were written during the Civil War, and though a handful wandered into print, the majority were hoarded from the sight of all but a few confidants until 1890, four years after her death, when the bulk of her work was issued in a collected edition and this wonderful poet stepped posthumously to the forefront of American poetry.

Her choice of anonymity, moreover, signaled a new

tendency among writers. By the end of the nineteenth century many had retired from society at large, distressed at how the radical mission of reshaping the world had been co-opted and transformed into bourgeois pieties. In Europe, industrial capitalism, spiritualized under the rubric of Christianity, had become the trademark of the post-revolutionary new man; Darwin's theory of evolution was appropriated and cheapened to justify ruthlessness, the new man bore the "white man's burden" into the dark heart of the Congo, into India, South America, the Caribbean. In this country Manifest Destiny celebrated the relentless trek to the Pacific, war on the Indian nations, and meddling in affairs south of the border; "Free Enterprise" translated into the seamy competition of Wall Street; democracy had deteriorated into jostling for wealth and status; power was fast becoming an ugly word; the bloom had faded from the youthful republic.

Many writers were saddened and appalled. No one articulated their dismay in clearer tones than Matthew Arnold, as in this passage from *Culture and Anarchy*:

Never did people believe anything more firmly than nine Englishmen out of ten at the present day believe that our greatness and welfare are proved by our being so very rich. Now, the use of culture is that it helps us, by means of its spiritual standard of perfection, to regard wealth as but machinery, and not only to say as a matter of words that we regard wealth as but machinery, but really to perceive and feel that it is so. If it were not for this

159

purging effect wrought upon our minds by culture, the whole world, the future as well as the present, would inevitably belong to the Philistines. The people who believe most that our greatness and welfare are proved by our being very rich, and who most give their lives and thoughts to becoming rich, are just the very people whom we call Philistines. Culture says: "Consider these people, then, their way of life, their habits, their manners, the very tones of their voice; look at them attentively; observe the literature they read, the things which give them pleasure, the words which come forth out of their mouths, the thoughts which make the furniture of their minds; would any amount of wealth be worth having with the condition that one was to become like these people by having it?"

The Writer in Retreat

The final decades of the nineteenth century saw in Paris and London "anti-social," certainly anti-majoritarian, movements of continuing influence. The French Symbolists favored poetry that bypassed mirrorings of nature or society and made a direct appeal to the senses, through rich allusive imagery and dreamlike language. Their precursor was Charles

Baudelaire, whose repellent visions of modern life, particularly of cities, opened the gates for an outpouring of poetry and fiction proudly at odds with the earnest hopefulness of the day. Baudelaire sees the poet as a man apart and therefore a hero, even a saint, who rejects a life of bland bourgeois malevolence. His best-known work is *Les Fleurs du Mal* (*The Flowers of Evil*). We saw one of its lyrics in "Voices of Prophecy." The chief Symbolists were Stéphane Mallarmé, Paul Verlaine, and literature's only bona fide prodigy, Arthur Rimbaud, who at sixteen wrote some of the most hypnotic poems in any language and at nineteen stopped writing for good. An offshoot of the Symbolists were the Decadents. The finest work produced by this movement was Huysmans's *Against Nature*, whose hero cultivates a life of consummate artificiality, surrounded by exotic perfumes and real flowers pruned to seem fake.

A parallel movement toward aestheticism dominated art and literature in *fin de siècle* England. Oscar Wilde was one proponent. Others were the printer and poet William Morris and the critic John Ruskin, who with his study of modern painters excited an entire generation. Poets like Swinburne and the Rossettis (Dante Gabriel and his sister Christina) were revulsed by the dogged respectability, complacency, and hearty optimism of Victorian England. Their verse, which explored the deeper regions of uncertainty and repression now commonly associated with their era, was accused in its time of morbid self-indulgence. The supreme novelist of this time was the

American expatriate Henry James whose huge output began in the last quarter of the nineteenth century and ended with his death in the early, tragic years of World War I. A rapt student of the subtle strategies of the mind, an avowed formalist, and far and away the best critic the novel has ever had, James pointed the way toward the movement that chiefly characterizes our own epoch—Modernism.

Modernism denotes the cosmopolitan gathering of composers, painters, and writers who resided in Paris during the first quarter of the twentieth century, and created an explosion of radical-seeming masterpieces, from Stravinsky's *Rites of Spring* to Picasso's *Les Demoiselles d'Avignon* to James Joyce's *Ulysses*. Modernism also includes London's Bloomsbury Circle, comprising painters (Duncan Grant, Vanessa Bell) and writers (Virginia Woolf, E. M. Forster) and even a seminal economist (John Maynard Keynes). Modernism includes Thomas Mann's monuments, in novels and essays, to a depleted culture; Franz Kafka's beautifully lucid pictures of the divided self; the oblique meditations of Wallace Stevens; William Faulkner's broodings over the abyss of history and the defeat of honor; and the prophetic poems of William Butler Yeats and Rainer Maria Rilke, Paul Valéry's 257 notebooks, and Proust's interior odyssey in search of lost time. With the exception of Yeats, born in 1865, each of the writers mentioned in this paragraph was born between 1870 and 1900. "Modernism," in short, designates the art and literature that resulted when the nineteenth century met the twentieth.

Some of the passages in "Illusion and Indulgence" come from Modernist works. Not only do they challenge inherited notions about what writing "should be"; they make the reader realize that what's before him is invented. In contrast to the spiritual or visionary side of literature stressed by the Romantics, Modernists were, with some notable exceptions, more interested in the form and shape their writing took. No longer voices speaking through language, they wanted words themselves, and the arrangement of a book's parts, to do all the speaking.

A feature of Modernism that may seem contrary to this obsession with form was its fascination with the subjective mind. An example of Modernist subjectivity: the passage by Faulkner in "Illusion and Indulgence." The scene it depicts—four persons riding in a car—is filtered through the recollecting mind of a single character for whom the event has multiple meanings. The sound and even the look of the words on the page suggest the inner workings of an aberrant mind in all its confusion and overlapping complexity. An experiment in form merges with a study of a consciousness, as if to prove that language can govern any subject.

A nonliterary precedent for such writing was set by Sigmund Freud, whose theories were becoming famous as this century began. More than any writer of the last hundred years, Freud, with his interest in dreams, his insistence that every gesture and word—jokes, faux pas, odd little compulsions—had meaning, sounded new depths in psychological writing. His own books, like the *Interpretation of Dreams*, and articles, "On Narcissism," "Mourning and Melancholia," and others, had an unmistakably mythic quality. All who read him closely understood that this Viennese psychoanalyst had contrived ingenious methods of interpretive reading. He also systematized the inner duality which had obsessed Western thought for three hundred years, and in terms so vivid that they are part of contemporary folklore. To the old contest between Good and Evil, Darkness and Light, Freud gave a new metaphor, medicinal or therapeutic, which lies behind the prevailing spiritual outlook of our day. Our forebears believed "weakness" and "sin" could be "conquered"; we believe that "aberration" and "illness" can be "cured."

The most important word in the literature of our century is "exile." There are several varieties of exile, and together they tell the story of the writer's relation to culture. The first is political: the modern era has seen the formation of totalitarian governments which, through censorship, imprisonment, or death have either silenced writers or chased them to the sanctuary of distant lands. Nazism drove Freud, Mann, the literary scholar and critic Walter Benjamin, Bertolt Brecht, the novelist and social critic Elias Canetti, and others out of Austria and Germany. The Russian Revolution uprooted Vladimir Nabokov, who migrated to England, France, and Germany, then to America, where he became our finest mid-century novelist before serenely passing his last days in the Swiss Alps; the poet Osip Mandelstam was not so lucky; he died in one of Stalin's death camps. Isaac Babel, perhaps the best short-story writer of the century, enjoyed a brief vogue in the Soviet Union before the authorities soured on him; he then suffered the painful comedy of beholding a mountain of "unprintable" manuscripts growing toward the ceiling before he, too, was thrown behind bars, where he shortly perished. As I write, Cuban poets and novelists languish in prison for "counterrevolutionary" activity and Czechoslovakian writers smuggle manuscripts to Paris and London.

A second kind of exile is not politically but morally motivated. Here our own country offers numerous examples. Henry James, who made literary capital out of his life abroad, put the case against his homeland succinctly:

> To make so much money that you won't, that you don't "mind," don't mind anything—that is absolutely, I think, the main American formula. Thus your making no money—or so little that it passes there for none—and being thereby distinctly reduced to minding, amounts to your being reduced to the knowledge that America is no place for you.

These words were written in the dawn of the "American century," when many of our most prized sensibilities were "reduced to minding." Ezra Pound, the prophet of Modernism, was born in Idaho, but lived most of his life in England and Italy. T. S. Eliot grew up in St. Louis, but after studying at Harvard crossed the ocean and, like James, became an English citizen, converting to Anglicanism and wearing each year a rose in his lapel commemorating the anniversary of Thomas Becket's "murder in the cathedral." Eliot, again like James, felt stifled by a tradition too thin for the "individual talent" aspiring to enter the canon of Western masters. No writer seems more American than Ernest Hemingway, yet he was schooled in war and writing in Europe, where he did his finest work. F. Scott Fitzgerald's overseas stint was briefer; it resulted, however, in *Tender Is the Night*, a rare American attempt at a Proustian novel. In our own day the enigmatic Thomas Pynchon has exiled himself from the world at large: he's unseen, unphotographed, unavailable for adulation.

Pynchon exemplifies a third variety of exile which, neither political nor moral, proclaims nothing. It seems instead self-protective, a fending off of irrelevant demands and expectations. When admirers traveled to Oxford, Mississippi, to catch a glimpse of Faulkner, he greeted them with a shotgun. J. D. Salinger, plagued by celebrity after *The Catcher in the Rye* and his popular story collections, disappeared into the New England woods, where he writes only for himself. Samuel Beckett continues to publish his cryptic work, but is an invisible voice speaking, furthermore, in an adopted language. Writers of the past were the spirits of their places; today they are displaced spirits, scattered by the diaspora of the "Generalised Life." The feeling one gets reading their work is not that they have deserted a home but that it has cast them out. Thus the century's most famous literary tourist, James Joyce (whose lone play is called *Exiles)*, carried a map of his native Dublin in his head.

Even those writers who stay at home evince estrangement. A feeling born in the last two centuries, that there is simply no public place for the serious writer, has reached a sorrowful fruition. The author's task, though, is unchanging. He must engage the mad and contradictory energies of the age; demonstrate the truth-dealing capacity of the imagination as knowledge continues to outstrip it; provide the conditions for attaining happiness at a time when we scarcely know what it means.

CONCLUSION:
BEING A READER

There was a time, as we have seen, when literature was more or less imbibed, a time of singing and listening. But once the author became a writer, forced to confront the strange demands of composition, his magic was transformed into a more complicated, ambiguous brand of legerdemain. For the audience, hearing was replaced by reading—the eye usurped the ear—and the bond between author and reader, no longer assured by the intimacy of performance, came to depend on a mutual puzzlement before language. The singing/hearing side of literature was not completely lost, of course. Indeed, among the illusions of literature the illusion of a "voice"—a human personality spontaneously uttering the words we read—is perhaps the most necessary.

We began with realistic fiction which, at every stage, was seen to refer back to the world of sociability. The point there was the interdependence of appearance and reality. Comic tellings of the oddities and impostures of public life disguised critical readings of human behavior, and simple tales conveyed bittersweet lessons. In passage after passage it grew clear that reality was hard to grasp cleanly. Often "reality" or "the truth" defined only one prejudiced or incomplete way of looking at things. This was especially apparent when we examined modern fiction, which recoiled from rendering any judgment of reality, and looked instead into the mind of the observer. There, in the interior world of impression and feeling, all meaning dwelt. Things as they are, are only things.

The inwardness of modern fiction took us to a new place: the long tradition of psychological writing, or literature of the mind. Freshly acclimated to passages that probed manners and morals, we were suddenly thrust onto a frontier of unsociability. In a series of selections at once suicidal and exultant, the very idea of community, of the "Generalised Life," was discovered to be inimical to sanity and self-preservation. We didn't blithely enlist in the misanthropic cause, but we did acknowledge that voices summoning us from the dark night of despair can be terribly alluring and rich with real complaint. In the drama of the mind, meaning is elusive. Death fantasies can conquer the suicidal impulse; mute resignation tolls certain doom.

It was reasonable that the next voices we heard spoke of the world being remade. The two kinds of literature we had just explored were now yoked together in moments of premonitory insight. Visionaries, it turned out, had both an inner and outer eye: they read the world in a large, cosmic way, yet fervently urged the validity of their private foretellings.

Here poets supplied us with the best material, perhaps because images are the natural conveyors of sudden illumination. Though not always specific about the precise shape of the unknown, poets deftly captured the sensations of alien landscapes. This feat extended further our initial experience of literature's essential ambiguity. For how could these poets *know*—well enough to describe it—the unknowable? How could they fashion with such completeness these cosmological inventories? The answer was that what seemed unimaginable was precisely its opposite: reality perceived through imagination. The visionary faculty is a regular part of our perceptive equipment, if only we trouble to use it.

After struggling with passages reeking of significance, it was refreshing to jump into a cool pool of nonsense. But again we had a problem. We had, perhaps unawares, grown addicted to meaning, to finding the deep germ of intention in everything we read. Nonsensical writing, totally subverting meaning, threw into disarray our most precious assumptions about literature. These playful put-ons, alas, had something serious to say. We ought to have guessed this immediately, for no activities are conducted more seriously than games, with their power to cancel the outside world. The passages we examined now rivaled, like dreams, the most basic assertions of "actual life."

We can now look back over the route we've traveled and see that, after all, it made sense. We began in the objective world of social reality; withdrew into the preoccupations of the interior self; voyaged to a place where, from the depths of solitude, new worlds seemed tangible; and arrived finally in the middle of those new worlds, only to discover that they had been built out of the oldest and most familiar tools in our possession—words. A direct journey, but also a circular one. It is origins, we learned, that all progress leads to.

This applies not only to the rival worlds of literature but also to their authors. Our quick historical run-through established that writers have never relinquished their membership in the human community, however much at odds with it they may be. They are citizens who contribute to the ongoing debate between revolution and tradition, culture and anarchy, between the tug of the future and the claims of the past. They are the antennae of the race, yet men and women apart. Our best listeners, they insist as well on being heard.

This book has tried to equip the reader for careful and sympathetic listening. I have assumed, from my opening pages, that reading is an activity, something we *do*, with energy and concentration, and with much at stake. Like love and friendship, reading is neither work nor relaxation. It belongs instead to that special place where all our disparate selves converge. Literature can provide us with revelation, or its mirror opposite, escape; it can give us both at once. At its most playful literature instructs, and when it is most urgent it disarms and delights.

Keeping these paradoxes in mind, the reader should be ready for anything, above all for surprise, the highest gift books can bestow and the motive behind their manifold deceits. Books mean to catch us up in our old selves, and offer us new ones. And they can only succeed when we are primed to become different people. It is we, in the end, who invent and inhabit the rival worlds of literature.

Appendix I: Notes

The page where the quotation first appears in the text is followed by bibliographical information.

5 Homer, *Odyssey*, trans. Robert Fitzgerald (Doubleday, Anchor Books, 1963), p. 119.

10 Northrop Frye, *The Great Code: The Bible and Literature* (Harcourt Brace Jovanovich, 1982), p. 7.

10 Aristotle, *Metaphysics*, trans. Richard Hope (Ann Arbor Paperbacks, University of Michigan Press, 1960), p. 265.

28 Samuel Johnson, "The Comedy of Romance," *Eighteenth Century Prose*, eds. Louis I. Bredvold, Robert K. Root, and George Sherburn (Thomas Nelson and Sons, 1935), pp. 485–88. (All subsequent Johnson quotations are from this source.)

22 Jane Austen, *Pride and Prejudice* (International Collectors Library), p. 78.

33 Charles Dickens, *Great Expectations* (International Collectors Library), p. 298.

36 Marcel Proust, *Swann's Way*, trans. C. K. Scott Moncrieff and Terènce Kilmartin (Random House, 1981), p. 235.

38 _____, *Within a Budding Grove* (same ed.), p. 465.

39 Lionel Trilling, "Cities of the Plain," *Speaking of Literature and Society*, ed. Diana Trilling (Harcourt Brace Jovanovich, 1980), p. 10.

41 Saul Bellow, *Herzog* (Viking Press, 1964), p. 201.

48 Raymond Carver, "What's In Alaska?" *Will You Please Be Quiet, Please? The Stories of Raymond Carver* (McGraw-Hill Paperbacks, 1978), p. 80.

53 William Shakespeare, *The Tragedy of King Richard the Second*, ed. Matthew W. Black (Penguin Books, 1972), V, v., 50.

54 Franz Kafka, *Diaries 1914–1923*, ed. Max Brod, trans. Martin Greenberg and Hannah Arendt (Shocken Paperbacks, 1968), p. 20.

58 Fyodor Dostoevsky, "Notes from the Underground," *Three Short Novels of Dostoevsky*, trans. Constance Garnett, rev. and ed. Avrahm Yarmolinsky (International Collectors Library), p. 138.

60 J. D. Salinger, "A Perfect Day for Bananafish," *Nine Stories* (Signet Books, 1959), p. 17.

61 Doris Lessing, "To Room Nineteen," *Stories* (Knopf, 1978), pp. 406–9.

64 Virginia Woolf, *A Room of One's Own* (Harcourt Brace Jovanovich, 1929), pp. 33–34.

67 Walt Whitman, "Song of Myself," *Leaves of Grass*, ed. Francis Murphy (Penguin Books, 1977), lines 69–83, pp. 66–67.

74 Joseph Conrad, *Nostromo* (Penguin Books, 1975), p. 409.

75 Friedrich Nietzsche, *Beyond Good and Evil*, trans. with commentary by Walter Kaufmann (Vintage, 1966), p. 15.

77 Robert Browning, "Childe Roland to the Dark Tower Came," *Poetical Works, 1833–1864*, ed. Ian Jack (Oxford Paperbacks, 1970), stanza XIII, p. 616.

79 Dante Alighieri, *Inferno*, with translation and comment by John D. Sinclair (Oxford University Press, 1974), canto XXV, pp. 308–11.

81 William Blake, "The Four Zoas," *The Poetry and Prose of William Blake*, ed. David V. Erdman, commentary by Harold Bloom (Doubleday, Anchor Books, 1970), "Night the First," lines 9–15, p. 297.

84 The Holy Bible, Authorized King James Version, Isa. 13.6–13.

86 William Butler Yeats, "The Second Coming," *Selected Poems and Two Plays of William Butler Yeats*, ed. M. L. Rosenthal (Macmillan, 1975), p. 91.

91 Charles Baudelaire, "La Béatrice," trans. Robert Lowell, *Les Fleurs du Mal* (New Directions, 1963), CXX, pp. 373–74.

100 James Joyce, *Ulysses* (Vintage, 1961), p. 383.

104 Tom Stoppard, *The Real Inspector Hound and After Magritte: Two Plays by Tom Stoppard* (Grove Press, 1977), pp. 15–16.

106 Oscar Wilde, "The Importance of Being Earnest," *The Portable Oscar Wilde*, rev. ed., ed. Richard Aldington and Stanley Weintraub (Viking Portable Library, 1981), Act I, p. 431.

107 Friedrich Nietzsche, *The Gay Science*, trans. with commentary by Walter Kaufmann (Vintage, 1974), pp. 96–98.

109 William Faulkner, "The Sound and the Fury," *The Faulkner Reader: Selections from the Works of William Faulkner* (Modern Library, 1946), p. 72.

112 George Herbert, "Easter Wings," *The English Poems of George Herbert*, ed. C. A. Patrides (Everyman's University Library, 1977), p. 63.

113 Alain Robbe-Grillet, "Jealousy," *Two Novels by Robbe-Grillet* (*Jealousy* and *In the Labyrinth*), trans. Richard Howard (Grove Press, 1965), p. 66.

145 Samuel Johnson, "The Life of Savage," *op. cit.*, p. 441.

154 John Keats, "To George and Georgiana Keats, 14–31 October 1818," *Letters of John Keats*, ed. Robert Gittings (Oxford Paperbacks, 1970), pp. 164–65.

157 Oscar Wilde, "To Mrs. Bernard Beere," 17 April 1882, *op. cit.*, p. 706.

159 Matthew Arnold, "Prose and Poetry," in *Culture and Anarchy*, ed. Archibald L. Bouton (Scribner, 1927), pp. 261–62.

165 Henry James, *The American Scene*, with introduction and notes by Leon Edel (Indiana University Press, 1968), p. 237.

Appendix II: Suggested Readings

The following lists are arranged chronologically, according to the author's date of birth. They make no pretense of completeness; they are, instead, entry points to a vast universe.

THINGS AS THEY ARE: THE REALISTIC NOVEL

Miguel de Cervantes, *Don Quixote*
Jonathan Swift, *Gulliver's Travels*
Henry Fielding, *Joseph Andrews, Tom Jones*
Voltaire, *Candide*
Jane Austen, *Sense and Sensibility, Pride and Prejudice, Emma*
Honoré de Balzac, *Eugénie Grandet, Père Goriot, Lost Illusions*
Victor Hugo, *Les Misérables*
William Makepeace Thackeray, *Vanity Fair*
Charles Dickens, *The Pickwick Papers, David Copperfield, Great Expectations, Bleak House*
Anthony Trollope, *Barchester Towers*
Ivan Turgenev, *Fathers and Sons*
George Eliot, *Adam Bede, Middlemarch*
Gustave Flaubert, *Madame Bovary, The Sentimental Education*
Leo Tolstoy, *War and Peace, Anna Karenina*
Mark Twain, *Huckleberry Finn*

Samuel Butler, *The Way of All Flesh*

Émile Zola, *Nana*, *Germinal*

Henry James, *The Portrait of a Lady*, *The Princess Casa-
massima*, *The Wings of the Dove*

Edith Wharton, *The Age of Innocence*

Marcel Proust, *Remembrance of Things Past*

Theodore Dreiser, *Sister Carrie*, *An American Tragedy*

Colette, *Chéri*, *La Fin de Chéri*

Ford Madox Ford, *The Good Soldier*

Thomas Mann, *Buddenbrooks*

E. M. Forster, *The Longest Journey*, *A Passage to India*,
Howard's End

F. Scott Fitzgerald, *The Great Gatsby*, *Tender Is the Night*

Ernest Hemingway, *The Sun Also Rises*

Christina Stead, *The Man Who Loved Children*

Evelyn Waugh, *Decline and Fall*, *A Handful of Dust*

Saul Bellow, *The Adventures of Augie March*, *Henderson the
Rain King*, *Herzog*

Nadine Gordimer, *Burgher's Daughter*

John Updike, *Rabbit, Run*; *Rabbit Redux*; *Rabbit is Rich*

Philip Roth, *Goodbye, Columbus*; *Letting Go*; *When She Was
Good*

Though not novels, these are splendid evocations of things as they
are:

Giovanni Boccaccio, *The Decameron* (prose tales)

Geoffrey Chaucer, *The Canterbury Tales* (in verse)

Baldassare Castiglione, *The Book of the Courtier* (dialogues)

Michel de Montaigne, *Selected Essays*

Madame de Sévigné, *Letters*

Duc de Saint-Simon, *Memoirs Cover the Years 1691–1723*

James Boswell, *The Life of Samuel Johnson, LL.D.*

Ivan Turgenev, *A Sportsman's Sketches* (stories)

Henrik Ibsen, *A Doll's House*, *Hedda Gabler*, *Ghosts*

Anton Chekhov, *Selected Stories*

James Joyce, *Dubliners* (stories)

Katherine Mansfield, *Bliss and Other Stories*
John Cheever, *The Stories of John Cheever*
Doris Lessing, *Stories*

MYSELF AM HELL: THE DIVIDED SELF IN LITERATURE

Homer, *Iliad* (epic poem)
Catullus, *Poems*
St. Augustine, *Confessions* (ruminations)
Geoffrey Chaucer, *Troilus and Criseyde* (narrative poem)
Christopher Marlowe, *Tamburlaine*, *Doctor Faustus* (plays)
William Shakespeare, *Richard II*, *Richard III*, *Hamlet*, *Oth-
    ello*, *Macbeth*, *Coriolanus*, *Antony and Cleopatra* (plays)
Pierre Corneille, *Le Cid* (play)
John Milton, "L'Allegro," "Il Penseroso" (poems)
Molière, *Tartuffe*, *The Misanthrope*, *Don Juan* (plays)
Blaise Pascal, *Pensées* (notes and ruminations)
Jean Racine, *Andromaque*, *Phèdre* (plays)
Jean-Jacques Rousseau, *Confessions* (memoirs)
Denis Diderot, *Rameau's Nephew* (dialogue)
Johann Wolfgang von Goethe, *The Sorrows of Young
    Werther*, *The Elective Affinities* (novels)
Heinrich Kleist, *Michael Kolhaus* (novel)
Stendhal, *The Red and the Black*, *The Charterhouse of Parma*
    (novels)
Lord Byron, *Don Juan* (poem)
Heinrich Heine, *Lyrics and Ballads*
Giacomo Leopardi, *Poems and Prose*
Nathaniel Hawthorne, *Twice-Told Tales*, *The Scarlet Letter*
    (novels)
Edgar Allan Poe, *Collected Stories*
Alfred Lord Tennyson, *Maud*, *In Memoriam* (poems)
Robert Browning, *Dramatic Romances and Lyrics*, *Men and
    Women* (poem collections)
Mikhail Lermontov, *A Hero of Our Time* (novel)
Charlotte Brontë, *Jane Eyre* (novel)
Emily Brontë, *Wuthering Heights* (novel)

Walt Whitman, *Leaves of Grass* (poem collection)

Herman Melville, *Bartleby the Scrivener, Billy Budd* (short novels)

Charles-Pierre Baudelaire, *The Flowers of Evil* (poem collection)

Fyodor Dostoevsky, *The Double, Notes from the Underground, Crime and Punishment* (novels)

Thomas Hardy, *The Mayor of Casterbridge* (novel)

Friedrich Nietzsche, *The Gay Science, Beyond Good and Evil, The Birth of Tragedy* (philosophical and aesthetic ruminations)

Sigmund Freud, "Mourning and Melancholia," "On Narcissism," "Repression," "Instincts and Their Vicissitudes" (essays); *Totem and Taboo* (four essays); *Case Histories* (short novels)

Joseph Conrad, *Lord Jim, Heart of Darkness, Under Western Eyes, Nostromo* (novels)

André Gide, *The Immoralist, The Counterfeiters* (novels)

Stephen Crane, *The Red Badge of Courage* (novel)

Robert Musil, *The Man Without Qualities* (novel)

James Joyce, *A Portrait of the Artist as a Young Man* (novel)

Franz Kafka, *Diaries, 1919–23*

D. H. Lawrence, *Sons and Lovers*, (novel)

Louis Ferdinand Céline, *Journey to the End of the Night, Death on the Installment Plan* (novels)

William Faulkner, *The Sound and the Fury, Light in August* (novels)

Jean-Paul Sartre, *Nausea, The Wall* (novels)

Elias Canetti, *Auto-Da-Fé* (novel)

Albert Camus, *The Stranger, The Fall* (novels)

Alberto Moravia, *The Conformist* (novel)

Ralph Ellison, *Invisible Man* (novel)

Saul Bellow, *Dangling Man, The Victim, Seize the Day* (novels)

Walker Percy, *The Moviegoer* (novel)

Robert Lowell, *Notebook, 1967–68* (poem collection)

James Baldwin, *The Fire Next Time* (essay)

Günter Grass, *The Tin Drum* (novel)
Italo Calvino, *The Cloven Viscount, The Nonexistent Knight* (novels)
V. S. Naipaul, *A Bend in the River* (novel)
Philip Roth, *Portnoy's Complaint* (novel)

VOICES OF PROPHECY: VISIONARY LITERATURE

The Bible: Books of Daniel, Isaiah, Revelation
Aeschylus, *The Oresteia, Prometheus Bound* (plays)
Sophocles, *Antigone, Oedipus the King, Oedipus at Colonus* (plays)
Euripides, *The Bacchae, The Trojan Women, Medea* (plays)
Virgil, *Aeneid* (epic poem)
Ovid, *Metamorphoses* (tales in verse)
Dante Alighieri, *The Divine Comedy* (epic poem)
Geoffrey Chaucer, *The Book of the Duchess* (poem)
Edmund Spenser, *The Faerie Queen* (epic poem)
William Shakespeare, *King Lear, Macbeth, Antony and Cleopatra* (plays)
John Milton, *Paradise Lost, Paradise Regained* (epic poems); *Samson Agonistes* (dramatic poem)
John Bunyan, *Pilgrim's Progress* (novel)
William Collins, *Odes* (poems)
William Blake, *Songs of Experience* (poem collection); *Jerusalem, Milton, The Four Zoas* (epic poems)
William Wordsworth and Samuel Taylor Coleridge, *Lyrical Ballads* (poem collection)
William Wordsworth, *Poems in Two Volumes, The Prelude* (autobiographical epic)
Percy Bysshe Shelley, *Prometheus Unbound* (dramatic poem); *Adonais* (elegy); *Odes*
John Keats, *Odes, The Fall of Hyperion* (dramatic poem)
Victor Hugo, *Odes and Ballads*
Ralph Waldo Emerson, *Collected Essays*
Nikolai Gogol, "The Overcoat" (short story)
Fyodor Dostoevsky, *The Brothers Karamazov* (novel)

Leo Tolstoy, *The Death of Ivan Ilyich* (short novel)
Emily Dickinson, *Poems*
Stéphane Mallarmé, *Hérodiade, The Afternoon of a Faun*
    (poems)
Henry James, *The Beast in the Jungle* (short novel); *The
    Wings of the Dove, The Ambassadors, The Golden Bowl*
    (novels)
Arthur Rimbaud, *Illuminations* (prose poems); *Season in
    Hell* (poem)
Peter Constantine Cavafy, *Poems*
William Butler Yeats, *Collected Poems*
Thomas Mann, *Tonio Kröger, Death in Venice* (short nov-
    els); *The Magic Mountain* (novel)
Rainer Maria Rilke, *Duino Elegies, The Sonnets to Orpheus*
    (poem sequences)
Wallace Stevens, *The Collected Poems*
Franz Kafka, *Metamorphosis, The Trial, The Castle* (novels),
    In the Penal Colony (stories)
William Carlos Williams, *Paterson* (five-volume poem)
D. H. Lawrence, *The Rainbow, Women in Love* (novels)
William Faulkner, *As I Lay Dying, The Sound and the Fury,
    Absalom Absalom!, The Wild Palms* (novels)
Bertolt Brecht, *The Threepenny Opera, The Jungle of Cities,
    Mother Courage, Galileo* (plays)
Federico García Lorca, *Poems*
Hart Crane, *The Bridge* (poem)
George Orwell, *1984* (novel)
Nathanael West, *Miss Lonelyhearts, The Day of the Locust*
    (novels)
Pablo Neruda, *Isla Negra* (poems)
Elizabeth Bishop, *The Complete Poems*
Bernard Malamud, *The Natural, The Assistant* (novels);
    The Magic Barrel (stories)
Norman Mailer, *The Deer Park*
Flannery O'Connor, *The Complete Stories*
Allen Ginsberg, *Kaddish* (poem collection)
James Merrill, *Divine Comedians* (poem collection)

John Ashbery, "Self-Portrait in A Convex Mirror" (poem); *Houseboat Days* (poem collection)

Robert Coover, *The Universal Baseball Association, Inc., J. Henry Waugh, Prop.* (novel)

Thomas Pynchon, *Gravity's Rainbow* (novel)

Sam Shepard, *The Tooth of Crime, The Buried Child* (plays)

ILLUSION AND INDULGENCE: LITERATURE AS A GAME

Aristophanes, *The Birds, The Frogs* (plays)

Petronius Arbiter, *The Satyricon* (novel)

Dante Alighieri, *The New Life* (poems and prose)

Petrarch, *Sonnets and Songs*

Geoffrey Chaucer, *The Parliament of Fowls* (poem)

Miguel de Cervantes, *Don Quixote* (novel)

William Shakespeare, *A Midsummer Night's Dream, Twelfth Night, The Tempest* (plays); *Sonnets*

John Donne, *Songs and Sonnets*

George Herbert, *The English Poems*

John Milton, *Comus* (verse play)

John Dryden, *Absalom and Achitophel, Mac Flecknoe* (poems)

Alexander Pope, *The Dunciad, The Rape of the Lock* (poems)

Jonathan Swift, *The Battle of the Books, A Tale of a Tub, Gulliver's Travels* (prose satires)

Laurence Sterne, *Tristram Shandy* (novel)

François René de Chateaubriand, *Atala, René* (prose epics)

Lord Byron, *Don Juan* (poem)

John Keats, *Lamia, Isabella, The Eve of St. Agnes, and Other Poems* (collection)

Alexander Pushkin, *Eugene Onegin* (verse novel); *Boris Godunov* (play)

Nathaniel Hawthorne, *The Marble Fawn* (novel)

Joris Karl Huysmans, *Against Nature* (novel)

August Strindberg, *The Dream Play, The Ghost Sonata* (plays)

Oscar Wilde, *Lady Windermere's Fan, The Importance of Being Earnest* (plays)

Gertrude Stein, *Three Lives* (novel)

Paul Valéry, *Selected Writings*

Virginia Woolf, *Mrs. Dalloway, To the Lighthouse, Between the Acts, The Waves, Orlando* (novels)

James Joyce, *Ulysses, Finnegans Wake* (novels)

Ezra Pound, *Pisan Cantos* (poem collection)

Marianne Moore, *Selected Poems*

T. S. Eliot, *Prufrock and Other Observations* (poem collection), *The Wasteland, Four Quartets* (poems)

Vladimir Nabokov, *Pnin, Lolita, Pale Fire* (novels); *Speak, Memory* (autobiography)

Jorge Luis Borges, *Ficciones, Labyrinths* (stories)

Nathanael West, *The Dream Life of Balso Snell* (novel)

Samuel Beckett, *Molloy, Malone Dies, The Unnameable* (novels); *Waiting for Godot, Happy Days, Endgame, Krapp's Last Tape, Rockaby* (plays)

John Cage, *Silence* (lectures and essays)

Alain Robbe-Grillet, *The Eraser, Jealousy* (novels)

Italo Calvino, *Cosmicomics, Invisible Cities, If on a winter's night a traveler* (novels)

Gabriel García Márquez, *One Hundred Years of Solitude* (novel)

John Barth, *Lost in the Funhouse* (stories); *Giles Goat-Boy* (novel)

Harold Pinter, *The Birthday Party, The Homecoming, No Man's Land* (plays)

John Updike, *The Centaur* (novel)

Tom Stoppard, *Rosencrantz and Guildenstern Are Dead, Jumpers, Travesties* (plays)

Appendix III: A Partial Bibliography

Here is a list of scholarly and critical works which were of particular assistance to me in preparing this volume, and which the reader may wish to examine for himself:

Abrams, M. H., *The Mirror and the Lamp: Romantic Theory and the Critical Tradition* (Oxford University Press, 1975), especially "Imitation and the Mirror" and "The Development of the Expressive Theory of Poetry and Art."

Barthes, Roland, *The Pleasure of the Text*, trans. Richard Miller (Hill & Wang, 1975).

Beckett, Samuel, *Proust* (Grove Press, 1931).

Blackmur, R. P., *A Primer of Ignorance*, ed. Joseph Frank (Harcourt Brace & World, 1967), especially "The Techniques of Trouble" and "The Logos in the Catacomb: The Role of the Intellectual."

Frye, Northrop, *Fables of Identity: Studies in Poetic Mythology* (Harcourt Brace & World, 1963), especially "Nature and Homer," "New Directions from Old," and "The Imaginative and the Imaginary."

_____ , *The Great Code: The Bible and Literature* (Harcourt Brace Jovanovich, 1982), especially "Language *I*."

Pirenne, Henri, *Economic and Social History of Medieval Europe*, trans. I. E. Clegg (Harcourt Brace & World, 1937), especially Part II, "The Towns."

Sennett, Richard, *The Fall of Public Man: On The Social Psychology of Capitalism* (Vintage Books, 1978), especially "Public Roles," "Public and Private," and "Man as Actor."

Sontag, Susan, *A Susan Sontag Reader* (Farrar, Straus & Giroux, 1982), especially "Against Interpretation," "Notes on Camp," and "The Aesthetics of Silence."

Tocqueville, Alexis de, *Democracy in America*, Vol. II (Knopf, 1946), especially chaps. XI-XXI.

Trilling, Lionel, *The Liberal Imagination* (Doubleday, Anchor Books, 1957), especially "Reality in America," "The Sense of the Past," "Manners, Morals, and the Novel," and "The Meaning of a Literary Idea."

_____ , *Sincerity and Authenticity* (Oxford University Press, 1974) especially, "The Honest Soul and the Disintegrated Consciousness" and "The Sentiment of Being and the Sentiments of Art."

Wilson, Edmund, *Axel's Castle: A Study in the Imaginative Literature of 1870–1930* (Charles Scribner's Sons, 1931, 1969).

INDEX

192

About the Author

Sam Tanenhaus holds degrees in literature from
Grinnell College and Yale University. A freelance
author and editor, he is currently a Junior Fellow
at the New York Institute for the Humanities. He
lives in Brooklyn, New York.